We Are All Fireflies is a blueprint for narrative-based counseling, not only for counselors but coaches and individuals as well. Written in a way the average reader can understand, with gripping stories and real-life examples, it will keep your attention while begging for you to look deep into yourself. Travis lays the groundwork for personal revelations and healing from past wounds that you may not have truly recognized before. The concepts shared in his book are going to change the way you examine your thought processes, and that could be life changing.

—Katy Seale

Travis engages with tenderness and rawness, drawing one into stories of humanity that uncover moments and feelings with courage few enter personally. But he doesn't leave it there. He invites us to journey with him into slivers of brokenness and oceans of healing that transcend our past stories and move us into creating new ones. *We Are All Fireflies* will inspire us to live abundant, present lives lit by lights of a hopeful future.

—Karen Kang
Creative Empowerment Coach

"Out of our darkest times comes our greatest achievement." Travis White captures the essence of this statement in *We Are All Fireflies*, a gripping story of childhood trauma. By sharing the challenging experience of living bound by his past, Travis whole-heartedly captivates readers with his personal testimony of courage, healing, and redemption. From the depths of darkness to finding light in his dreams, Travis uses his inspirational voice to spin hope into the heart of others. As a tool to help readers overcome limiting beliefs, this book reminds us that we do not have to do this journey alone and the past does not have to define us.

—Author and Wellness Educator, Hope Flansburg

As a counselor, I recognize the power of being a wounded healer and knowing our own story so we can help others. When we allow ourselves to see our unconscious—the pain, the anguish, the despair—we find our true selves in the process. This book resonates with my novel, *The Beckoning Rooms*, in that the protagonists all must go through a grueling process of discovery to heal and know who they are. Travis does this in his journey. Healing is all about mindset, and Travis's book will help us make the adjustments in our thinking to heal the wounds of the past and enable us to move forward to a freer, brighter future. The best thing is, with counseling to help, you need not do it alone. Travis's message will bring people to recognition, acceptance, empowerment, and forward movement despite the memories and pain of the past. My motto is *let's get this life back on track*, and I believe *We Are All Fireflies* will help readers do just that.

—Karin Brauner
Counselor, Supervisor, and Coach at <u>www. karinbrauneronline.co.uk</u>.Author of *20 Self-care Habits: Develop Your Strengths, Use Your Resources, and Improve Your Life and Relationships*, and *The Beckoning Rooms: Deal with Them or they will Deal with You.*

We overcome childhood trauma by shedding light on it instead of letting it fester in the darkness. In *We Are All Fireflies*, author Travis White, who has overcome the ravages of childhood sexual abuse, faces his struggles head-on with courage and sensitivity. He takes us on his journey from the pain and long-term damaging effects of the trauma to self-discovery, hope, and overcoming. This extraordinary book inspires, encourages, and empowers the reader. Travis teaches us the value of seeking counseling and shows us how to go from victim to victor by choosing our internal dialogue and changing what we believe, focus on, and think. Read *We Are All Fireflies* to become the master of your fate and claim the freedom and joy you thought you could never have.

—Dr. Sandra E. Duclos, Clinical Psychologist
President, Sandra E. Duclos, Ph.D., Inc.
Author, *Waiting for Luigi*

A unique blend of counselor and coach, Travis takes the reader on a healing journey with *We Are All Fireflies*. If you ever find yourself fortunate enough to sit across from him in a coffee shop, you will be enlightened. Travis is in the business of changing lives by changing stories. Through his brave vulnerability, he walks you through a clear process for lasting transformation.

—Brenda A Haire, Author of Save the Butter Tubs!:
Discover Your Worth in a Disposable World.

With the power of words, immense transparency, and vulnerability, Travis uses the trauma of his past to enlighten and encourage us to embrace our narrative in *We Are All Fireflies*. Travis guided me to embrace the good news- I can continue to live in my past narrative or practically find my inner light and live my best life; the one waiting right around the corner. He guided me through the journey with a perfect mix of pain, humor, and healing to help me reach my destination and live a fuller life, embracing my inner light and living, truly living! *We Are All Fireflies* is a must read.

—Melissa Salmon, Marketing, Copy, and Content Writer – beejoyfulsolutions.com

WE ARE ALL
FIREFLIES

We Are All Fireflies

Finding Your Light In The Darkness

Travis M White

Published by Author Academy Elite
PO Box 43, Powell, OH 43065
www.AuthorAcademyElite.com

Identifiers:

LCCN: 2021923233

ISBN: 978-1-64746-965-8 (paperback)
ISBN: 978-1-64746-966-5 (hardback)
ISBN: 978-1-64746-967-2 (e-book)

Available in paperback, hardback, and e-book

To my precious family,

I could not have found my light and healing had you not been the most amazing, supportive, and patient people in my life. I love you.

To all my friends/clients who have journeyed with me,

Thank you for the love, grace, and support you have given me through the years. I am blessed that you have chosen to include me in part of your stories.

To you, the reader,

Thank you for purchasing my book. I pray that it brings clarity to you or someone you love. May it bring light to whatever darkness you struggle with.

**We carry all the light we will ever need
to illuminate all the darkness we will ever face.**

CONTENTS

Part One
Redeeming Your Past

Part Two
Reclaiming Your Present

Part Three
Reimagining Your Future

FOREWORD

I believe that everyone lives a story worth sharing, and whether good times or bad, victories or struggles, every story has the potential to bless and guide others. In *We Are All Fireflies,* Travis gives us a front-row seat on his journey from the bondage of darkness birthed in childhood sexual abuse and into the light of the freedom and healing he found in discovering his true worth. More than just a biography of one man's life story, this book is a guide for anyone dealing with the effects of past trauma or personal pain.

I met Travis two years ago when he attended his first Igniting Souls Conference, and I am honored to be publishing his first book. He is a warm, heart-filled soul that I would call a wounded healer, meaning he knows pain but lives life as an overcomer. Unlike many personal growth and self-help books, Travis does not paint the steps of his journey as easy or without struggle. Rather, he goes into detail as he shares the internal battle with fear, shame, and anxiety that plagued him for much of his life. With an inspiring level of vulnerability, you will follow Travis, not only on the path that led to his ultimate freedom and healing but also through the missteps and mistakes made along the way. He truly shines a light into his darkness, hoping others may endure less pain and setback in their journeys.

Travis reveals how, in every moment and every experience of our lives, we are writing our personal stories. Most of the time, we write pretty good ones, but sometimes we endure pain or trauma that leads us to write and believe in painful chapters we would rather forget. "*Words create worlds*" is a mantra Travis repeatedly refers to throughout his book. He explains how the story we believe about ourselves will influence and guide the way we live. Learning to experience our best lives is greatly dependent on learning to master what he calls our internal narrative.

Through poignant and personal life experiences and lessons, Travis's approach makes you feel as if you are part of an intimate conversation rather than reading a cold, prescriptive list of techniques to implement. While sharing the process he adopted to find freedom and healing, Travis is quick to point out that every journey through pain or trauma is unique and personal. He hopes his story will awaken others to the narrative inside and help them understand how past experiences can hack our identity and self-belief. Not wanting to leave us at the point of newfound freedom and healing, wondering what to do next, Travis outlines eight helpful personal mindsets to adopt into our daily lives to keep us on the path of meaning and purpose.

We Are All Fireflies is an inspiring look into the journey from darkness to light. I believe it will prove to be an excellent resource for anyone wanting to experience more in life and find freedom from bondage, possibly bondage you never understood until reading this book. Travis believes we all have the power to find our best selves. As the opening quote in his book says, "You carry all the light you will ever need to illuminate all the darkness you will ever face." Get ready to be encouraged and motivated to discover your best life.

— Kary Oberbrunner, *Wall Street Journal* and *USA Today* bestselling author, and CEO of Igniting Souls Publishing Agency

A NOTE TO THE READER:
THE DUALITY OF BELIEF

It was not easy getting to a place where I could share my story in a book like this. Parts of the journey were downright brutal. There was also plenty of beauty. If given the choice, wouldn't we want to focus on the beauty, on the good things in life? But, one of the main things I have learned in getting here is that we need to deal with the hard things. They demand, in one way or another, to be dealt with.

Let me start with one of those hard things. One of the key constructs we will discuss in chapter four is also one of the main barriers that almost prevented me from sharing my story: belief. Although I had already overcome a crisis of belief on my journey, the struggle was reborn when I considered publishing this book.

Belief is one of the most powerful forces in the universe. It can hold you in a dark place of bondage, and it can ignite your soul into a beautiful place of freedom and redemption. For me, it did both. Those old, defeated demons tried to resurrect themselves in my inner thoughts:

Who would want to read this book?

Do you really think your story is going to help anyone?

You know you cannot share it with others unless it is perfect and accepted by everyone. In the past, I would have gotten stuck right there. I would have retreated, licked my wounds, and added that failure to the long list of burdens I carried for not believing in myself.

Words fuel our beliefs, including the words we read, hear, and, most of all, the words we speak to ourselves. That inner dialogue, or inner narrative, as I call it, is what moves us forward or paralyzes us with the belief that we will never fully experience the life we long for.

The focus of this book is our internal narrative. It is my passion to help people understand just how powerful words are. In our information-saturated age, words have become cheap. Sure, we still have beautiful stories, songs, and poems, but much of our culture throws around words without giving thought to their immense power. Remember that popular playground mantra, "Sticks and stones can break my bones, but words will never hurt me." Oh, how wrong that sentiment is. Words can build kingdoms and tear down walls. They can incite war, and they can bring peace. Words can lift a person to accomplish their greatest dreams, and they can tear them down to the point of brokenness.

I allowed my own internal narrative to hold me in bondage for forty years. The words I spoke about painful things in my childhood created a destructive and debilitating story. The longer I listened to it and believed in it, the worse things became. Over a long period, full of many struggles and failures, I learned to embrace a new story, a story that freed me from bondage and restored the light of peace and joy in my life. My words eventually helped me to embrace the world I knew God had planned for me all along. *We Are All Fireflies* will take you on that journey from darkness to light.

It has been a painful but healing process to gain the courage to share my story. I have felt grossly inadequate. I have fought the voice that has tried to tell me, *No one wants to hear your story*, or *who do you think you are, giving people life advice?* There has been continual inspiration and encouragement from God, family, and friends speaking to me amid it all. While I share a lot of what I have learned about the science behind thoughts, feelings, and emotions, I do not profess to be an expert on the brain. You will also note that I share a lot about how God has spoken to me, but I do not present myself as a thought leader in the field of theology either. Instead, I have written this book from the point of view from which I have the most experience and expertise, my own story. I have had a first-class ticket to the pain of sexual trauma in my childhood. There is an intimate connection to the destructive narratives formed around my story. I have witnessed the train wrecks of the poor choices I had made while in bondage to fear and shame, as well as the hurt I caused those who loved me most.

Why would you want to read a story of freedom and light from a person who struggled with bondage and darkness for almost two-thirds of his life? Well, because I struggled with bondage and darkness for almost two-thirds of my life. Struggl*ed*, as in past tense. And if I can do it, then you can, too. *It is not too late for you!*

I have learned a lot on my journey. Yes, I held onto fear and shame longer than I should have. Yes, it took me forty years to ask for help. Yes, I made a lot of mistakes along the way. But I pressed on, learned from my experiences, and grew as a person. I was very accident-prone as a kid; my dad used to joke that I didn't just fall off the ladder, I hit every rung on the way down. That summarizes my journey to the place I am now. Whether due to bad luck or a thick skull, I tend to learn the hard way. I have had almost every experience imaginable on my journey to freedom and healing, so I find I can relate to most people when we begin to share war stories. If sharing my story can help just one person avoid at least one struggle I endured, it will be worth it.

I want everyone to know freedom from whatever bondage or pain they may be experiencing. I want everyone to have the opportunity to chase their dreams and embrace their best life.

This book is for you, if

- you think there must be more to life than what you are experiencing now.

- you struggle to believe in yourself or your hopes and dreams.

- you know the pain and bondage that come from childhood trauma.

- you feel stuck at the point of your greatest failure or mistake.

If you live with the burden of hopelessness, fear, shame, anxiety, or believing you will never be enough, please know there is freedom and hope. Your best life awaits you. Now is the time to find your way out of whatever darkness ensnares your life. Now is the time to find your inner light. Why wait? You deserve it, and the world needs your light.

INTRODUCTION
TRAIN WRECKS, FIREFLIES, AND
MERRY-GO-ROUNDS

Tell your story: yes, tell your story! Give your example.
Tell everyone that it's possible, and other people will
then have the courage to face their own mountains.

—*Paulo Coelho*

I needed some clarity. Sitting at a table in one of my favorite coffee shops, I wrestled with the sudden explosion of thoughts and emotions bouncing around inside me. I had intended to journal to help make sense of things, but my thoughts refused to flow. Pain overwhelmed me. Darkness surrounded me. Part of me wanted to cry, and the other part wanted to scream at the top of my lungs. I wanted to be left alone, but I also wanted someone to grab me, hold me, and tell me it was all going to be okay.

I was at a crossroad.

In one direction lay a dark past I had never dealt with, and in the other, a train wreck of destruction I had caused. I pictured myself sitting on the ground where the two roads met. I felt lost, and I didn't know where to turn.

Some days, the coffee shop provided a peaceful quiet to think alone. Other days, it brought just the right friend to my table. This day, a friend came. He sat down and, after some small talk about the weather and the last good book we'd each enjoyed, he asked me how things were going.

It seemed an honest and open invitation to truly share, rather than the usual sterile gesture that expects a clipped, reassuring response. We had not crossed paths in quite some time, and I could not help but think God had led him here to connect with me. This friend always had the kind of heart to respond to things like that.

I struggled to capture the words swimming around in my head, and instead, I broke down in tears. For several minutes, I just cried, but in his silence, I could sense he was listening. My mouth slowly started to form words, and I shared with him the brokenness I was experiencing. I shared about the poor choices I had made and how I had hurt those closest to me. And, before I knew it, I was sharing about the darkest parts of my childhood. Sharing my story—my mistakes and broken past—was painful and empowering at the same time. Speaking about my darkness with another person was something I had rarely done. I had so many questions:

Why did I feel so unworthy to be heard?
Why did I have so much fear and shame about my past?
Why was I struggling to share when sharing is what I help others do?

Most of the time, when I even considered talking about my past, I shut down. It stirred too much fear. Words and memories painted pictures I felt powerless to face, powerless to free myself from. Unworthiness was always my default feeling when trying to share my story and pain with others. It felt odd that I could not do what I guided others to do during coaching sessions. I encourage people to be honest and open to others' support. But when it came to my pain and struggles, I usually resolved to carry my burden alone. I treated my clients and friends as if they deserved something that I did not.

But that day proved different. My friend's receptive spirit allowed me to utter the word I had felt unworthy of speaking my whole life.

Help.

As tears streamed down my face, soaking into the pages of my journal, I looked up at my friend and said, "I need help." A simple statement, yet it felt like the hardest thing I had ever done. It's like that for a lot of us.

My friend listened and wept with me. He made me smile when he could sense me buckling under the weight of the veil of darkness that I was struggling to pull back. In one of those moments, the heavy words of pain gave way to the joyful remembrance of time spent chasing fireflies as a child. I spent many a summer night sitting under the big pecan trees, watching the fireflies. Sometimes there were so many of them, their lights looked like fireworks floating on the thick, humid Texas air.

I often collected them in a jar and put them in my bedroom window at night. I would watch them glow in the dark, hoping they would take away my fears, but their light never protected me from the darkness. That was the end of the pleasant memory of fireflies. Our conversation snapped back to the reality of me being so afraid as a child.

When I described the fireflies as my failed saviors, my friend then spoke the words which would ignite my soul on the journey I had desired and needed for forty years. He shared how the light from the fireflies was never meant to protect me from my own darkness. That light belonged to them. It had power for them, but not for me. Then he said to me, "What if you are the firefly, and you've just lost the connection to your own light?"

He was right. I wept over how true that statement felt. I was living in a place of darkness that my words and memories had created. Here I was with a beautiful life I never felt worthy of, while being constantly pursued by a past life I believed I could not overcome.

This place had become familiar as I had been here more times than I can remember, where I wrestled with the need to share my story, wondering if anyone would care. I struggled with what people would think about me and the hard truths of my experiences, or whether they would find value in the things I had learned. Like I had done for much of my life, I questioned my worth based on my assumptions about what others would think of me. And that belief kept me in bondage.

A good portion of my life entailed battling the pain of my past while fighting to create the life I longed for. I worked hard to love my family, help others, and have value in life. But I was doing it all from a deep belief that nothing would ever help me overcome the fear and shame of my past. It's as if I were moving a hundred miles an hour through life while feeling completely stuck. The crazy image popped into my head of someone so excited to go on a grand adventure, but then choosing a merry-go-round as the mode of transportation. There was a lot of movement in my life, a lot of effort, but I was getting nowhere. Crazy, right?

But no more. Here I was, now vulnerably embracing and courageously sharing my story. There was no turning back.

What was different about this time? *Me.* I finally found the courage to see things as they were. As I shared the words of my story with my friend, I noticed a pattern emerge. I wondered if I had never noticed it before or if I was too afraid to acknowledge its presence. Looking back, I believe it was a combination of the two. The pattern was simple. I was the sole source of my bondage. It was not my past. It was not the terrible things that had happened to me, nor the poor choices I had made. It was me. I had convinced myself to be afraid of my past while also fearing everything that held the power to set me free.

This painful but empowering awareness allowed me to experience, for the first time, the true nature of brokenness. I know; brokenness sounds so painful, hopeless even. But I have learned it is the backbone of the courage to move forward. It became clear to me that vulnerability is not to be feared; rather, it fuels movement and growth. I had been in bondage most of my life because I feared the process of discovering freedom. I feared I was powerless. I feared being stuck sitting at that dark crossroad my whole life. Now was the time for my awakening.

Are you ready for yours? Are you ready to stop hiding, stop letting fear control you, stop believing that suffering is just a part of your life? I'm here to tell you it can happen!

Join me on the journey of redeeming your past, reclaiming your present, and reimagining your future, so you too can fully and freely embrace the life you long for.

PART ONE

Redeeming
Your Past

Awakening: A revival of interest or coming into awareness of something. Awakening is about making an intimate connection with the story we all carry inside us.

The good parts of our stories are easy to remember. We enjoy recalling them and experiencing the emotions we felt in those moments. But what do we do with the painful parts? What happens to the trauma, the moments we were afraid, or the times we didn't have answers for what we were feeling or experiencing? For most people, the answer is to bury them away, hoping we can forget them. But, like cancer or a virus, those hidden words are the ones that usually cause the most damage. These first four chapters are about bringing our stories into the light, uncovering the painful narratives holding us in bondage, and realizing our potential for finding freedom.

Here's the deal: This process is not easy, but as I said before, it is beautiful. Freedom comes in fully knowing yourself. If you struggle with past trauma or hold on to past pain, I know there are pages or chapters of your stories you would like to rip out. I get it. I was once there. I share my personal experiences in Part One, not because I want sympathy, but because I want you to see that everything you have gone through in your life has the potential to teach and grow you. That is a truth that took me a long time to learn. Everything you fear and everything you think is impossible to overcome holds the keys to finding the freedom you desire. Every choice, failure, and bad thing you endured can all bring redemption.

Our stories will either write us, or we will write our stories. Step bravely into yours as we journey together through this process of awakening.

1

DISCOVER

The Presence of Narrative

When we deny the story, it defines us.
When we own the story, we can write a brave new ending.
—*Brené Brown*

It was a typical summer day in Texas—sunny, hot, and so humid you could almost cut the air with a knife. It was also a great day to roll the windows down, turn up the radio, and go riding around in the countryside. When our son was little, he loved taking long rides to nowhere with his Pop (my dad). On this beautiful day, large puffy clouds floated like cotton candy in the sky's bright blue background.

If you've ever lived in Texas, you know the weather can change instantly. Those puffy clouds piled up on the horizon until they became dark, ominous storm clouds. My son, being caught up in the deep conversation with his Pop about the latest adventure on his toy four-wheeler, failed to notice—until a loud thunderclap startled him. Wide-eyed, he watched lightning dance across the sky. Looking at the clouds and then at Pop, he asked, "Are we going to have a tornado? Should we go back home?" My dad looked over at my son who had hunched fearfully down in his seat, and told him, "We don't have to worry about those storm clouds buddy; they are way off in the distance." He looked at his Pop and back out the window at the tall, dark clouds and proclaimed, "Pop, *distance* sure is a scary word."

Our family cracks up every time we recall this story. It's cute when kids use language in unexpected ways. But the story also contains a core truth I learned on my journey from darkness to light: Words create worlds.[1] While *distance*, by definition, is a simple, harmless word, in my son's imagination, it evoked a frightful world full of lightning, thunder, and tornadoes. As a little boy, it just made sense that if the scary storms were in the distance, then distance must be something to be feared as well. This world he created in his mind with his words stayed with him for quite some time. Until he learned better, he often felt afraid every time he saw storm clouds (you know the rest) off in the distance.

Awareness of Our Narrative

When our words stir joy and happiness rather than fear, the worlds we create are easy to embrace. As I described the sunny day shared by my dad and son, maybe you recalled your own similar world of experience. For me, words like *purple-hulled peas* take me back to my grandmother, wearing a dress and apron, cooking in the kitchen. I cannot hear the word *train* without thinking about the long Saturday walks that my grandfather and I took up and down backcountry stretches of railroad. When I hear the word *fishing*, I recall the days my dad and I spent in a boat together. But other words can create worlds full of hurt, fear, and pain. What do we do with those?

Many of us hide those words and the stories they force us to remember. No one likes to hurt. No one likes to think about the things we fear. So, we shut those parts of our stories down. When we have experiences that remind us of the painful parts of our past, we tend to avoid, deny, or get lost in (often destructive) habits or coping mechanisms. If you are a man reading this book, you know what we do best. We lock those memories and worlds away in the dark recesses of our minds. We do not like to deal with things we cannot fix. Am I right, guys?

What's the problem with ignoring the painful parts of our past? Don't we deserve to be happy? Sure, we do. But ignoring the parts of your narrative that are painful is like tearing pages out of a novel and expecting it to still make sense. It doesn't work. As hard as it is to recall past trauma, fears, or painful memories, I have learned they hold just as much value for us as the good times. Yes, I said it: the painful parts of our past are just as important as the good parts in helping us grow and become the person we long to be. Let me be honest and say that I struggled with believing this for much of my life.

While we will look at those good memories head-on, most of us take a side glance, at best, when our minds awaken to the darker parts of our past. I have learned, though, that one key to finding myself, to knowing true freedom, was to be fully aware of this internal narrative that I carry around. You cannot know complete freedom in life until you understand what keeps you in bondage. A lot of struggles we have with anxiety, shame, lack of self-worth, and a myriad of other issues find their source in the stories we come to believe about who we are. Most of us will wrestle with these surface issues without ever getting to the root of the why, what, where, and how of the inner narratives fueling those struggles.

To truly understand the novel, we must read all the pages of the story. To truly understand ourselves, we must awaken and embrace the full narrative that we have written throughout our lives. This means we must work to make the unconscious conscious. It is not easy, but it is vital to us knowing real freedom and complete joy and peace.

Fear and the Big Question

For as long as I can remember, before my healing journey, I was always afraid. As a man, that fear has been a very humbling thing to admit. We learn to be tough, to stand strong, and to never fear. Let me just say, that is very destructive teaching for men and women alike. We are human. We struggle. Everyone needs to ask for help at times. And until we face our fears and our past pain, we will continue to operate under their shadows and their power will continue to disrupt our lives.

I thought being afraid was part of my destiny; something I was meant to endure while being determined to hide it from the rest of the world. I mean, how does this sound: husband, father, friend, athlete, military veteran, competitive person, country boy, and *scaredy-cat*? Every time I found myself lost in whatever cloud of fears I faced in life, I felt anxious, hopeless, and as if I had no value in the world. Can you relate? I didn't want to face that part of who I was, so I avoided it, denied it, and at times, struggled with medicating it (we will talk about that in a later chapter). But, after my wife and I endured a huge train wreck in our marriage, I had had enough. I was tired of feeling less than others and like I didn't belong. And I was broken by who it had made me become. I had spent too many years focused on creating the facade of this perfect life narrative and had avoided the painful, traumatic truths that inhabited my story. Allowing myself to exist in bondage to my fear almost destroyed me.

The courage to call out those fears finally came when I was sitting on a large boulder on the side of a mountain in Tennessee, as the events of my past were running through my head on repeat. I was crying out in pain and anger at God and myself. "Why did I have to endure sexual abuse as a child? Why did it take me so long to ask for help? Why did it take a life-altering mistake to wake me up?" As my words echoed across the side of the mountain, the one question flowed out of my mouth that would change everything for me. At the top of my lungs, I yelled out, "What are you so f-ing afraid of?"

Silence. My breathing grew heavy, and tears began streaming down my face. I knew the answer as soon as I asked the question:

I am afraid that I am worthless and unlovable.

What? Where did that come from? I have a great life, a great marriage, amazing kids, and tons of friends. My life is full of blessings. I had two extremely loving parents. But the words hung on the air and in my heart like a lead balloon. There it was, my greatest fear, staring me straight in the face.

What do you fear most in life? The answer to that question could be the beginning of finding the freedom you long for. It was for me. Every client I work with hears this question. Contemplating the answer is often met with confusion and sometimes with tears. The most common first answer is, "I don't know." But almost everyone I work with eventually realizes, as I did, that they carry a core fear that causes much of the pain and problems in their lives. Whether it be past trauma, relationship struggles, mental health issues, or a feeling of being stuck in life, much of the power these things have over us is rooted in the words we speak in our own minds. The most destructive narratives are those rooted in fears born out of past trauma that we never processed.

So, what do we do with the parts of our stories we would rather forget? If we listen to the world, we often hear advice like this: "Just quit thinking about the painful parts and be happy." "That happened a long time ago, get over it." "The past is the past; you cannot change it."

If you have ever endured any kind of trauma, please do not listen to advice like this. Sure, it may have happened a long time ago. Of course, we want to live our lives and be happy. But here's the deal: when our mind tries to make sense of trauma while still experiencing it, we are often overcome with lies and destructive ideas because we are trying to make sense of things amid the chaos. Until we correct those narratives, we will struggle with those beliefs.

The Greatest Trauma

I have learned that trauma is less about the "what" of our experience and much more about the story we write about it. For most of us, the trauma ends at some point, but the story endures. Whatever we believed in the moment of fear or pain will go with us until we challenge and change that narrative. The greatest trauma is not *what* happened to us, but what it caused us to *believe* about ourselves.

Remember my biggest fear: I am worthless and unlovable. There has never been any part of my past lost or blocked out of my mind. I remembered all the good times, and I remembered the sexual abuse I went through, but I could not put my finger on where this fear was born. That is until I started this process of awakening to the whole of my narrative. I recall asking myself over and over, *can you remember a time that you felt worthless and unlovable?* The memories came slowly at first, but then they flooded my mind with the awareness that I had believed this about myself for much of my life. Why is this important? I mean, it's not fun to recall the painful things. I would have rather been doing anything else in the world. But how can we challenge an internal narrative that we do not fully understand?

Being afraid was the theme of the first six years of my life. As a small child, the fear centered on the belief that I couldn't take care of my mother. She divorced my biological father when I was about three or four, but he would still come around, usually when he was drunk. He was very loud and abusive toward my mother, and I remember wanting to be brave and help her. But I just lay in bed, too afraid to move, until the yelling stopped, and everyone went to sleep.

One night, after it got quiet, my father came into my room. I pretended to be asleep, but I could see out of the corner of my eye he had picked up the jar of fireflies I had in my bedroom window. I could smell the stale alcohol and cigarettes on his breath as he talked about how sweet of a boy I was. And then, he sexually assaulted me. I would rather spare you the gory details, but it devastated me. It happened on at least two more occasions. After a short time, my father stopped coming around, and my mom met and married another man. It turns out that he was also an alcoholic and very abusive. I am not sure whether he perpetrated at least one of my sexual abuse incidents. I only know something very bad happened that suddenly ended their brief marriage. One hot summer day, I came into the house to hear him and my mom yelling at the top of their lungs. I don't recall what they were talking about, but he went to the closet, pulled out a gun, and held it to her face. All I could think was how helpless I was to protect my mother. He stepped back and went around to the other side of the bed and then held the gun to his own head. For some reason, he just passed out and fell to the floor. Mom grabbed my infant sister and an armload of belongings, and we left.

She Smiled

My mother was young and doing her best to take care of my sister and me. I have never blamed her for the type of men she met and brought into our lives. Besides, all that bad luck was about to change. Mom worked hard at an army ammunition plant and spent most of her free time caring for us. But one day, she came home and told me she was taking us to the babysitter's house because she had a date. I cried the whole way there. I hated that house, and terror filled my mind at the thought of staying there. I told you: I was afraid of everything. Besides, I was six years old and felt too big to go to a babysitter. She gave in to my tantrum and took me with her on her date. We drove to a roadside park outside of our hometown of Marshall, where she was to meet this guy. I was nervous as we got out of the car. I did not trust men very much at this point in my life.

We walked over to the coolest car in the park, a shiny Ford Mustang. When the door opened, the sounds of Elvis Presley filled the air, and out stepped a man with the most welcome smile I had ever seen. He shook my hand and said hello to me before hugging my mom. He wore black-rimmed glasses and had sideburns down to his jawline that framed his Buddy Holly look. I couldn't stop staring at him. My mom interrupted the moment and told me to go play on the swings. After all, they were on a date.

As I watched them talk and hug and giggle, it happened. She smiled. Something he said made her smile. This was a huge thing because I rarely remember her smiling for the first six years of my life. I am sure she did, but I remember mostly pain and sadness. I tell you this story for a reason. This is one of the memories that arose in my thoughts as I recalled all the different times my core fear stirred. I would soon discover this was *the* time, *the* moment, that narrative was born in my story.

Even as a child, I took it upon myself to take care of my mom, to make her happy. I had failed. As I watched this man make her smile, guilt riddled my thoughts. *How could he do something so easily that I had never been able to do?* I wasn't jealous or angry at him, instead I felt enamored with him. I had a feeling this could be the man who would make Mom happy and care for our family. As I imagined what it would be like to have him as my dad, a deep, inexplicable dread came over me. This man is special. He is kind and caring. He makes her happy. Why did I feel dread, then? Because I did not feel worthy of being loved by a man like him. I did not feel worthy of my mom because I had not protected her. I somehow reckoned the abuse and failure of both her marriages were my fault. I could not let him know my story or he might leave us. Crazy, right? There's that narrative we spoke about when we try to make sense out of chaos. I decided then and there that I would hide my story; I was too afraid to face it. As I watched her continue to smile, I decided I would replace my painful narrative with good. I would spend my life doing what this man did for my mom, making people smile and making them happy. To do that, there was no way I could share my darkness. So, into the abyss, it went.

Identity Hack

It was a hot summer Saturday, and I was spending the day at my grandparent's house. I had just gotten off my bike in the front yard when I heard that sound that puts a smile on every kid's face: the ice cream truck. I burst into the house loudly exclaiming, "Me-Me, the ice cream man is coming! Can I have some money for the ice cream man, please?" She gently responded, "Travis Michael, what did I tell you about using your inside voice?" She smiled and gave me fifty cents.

I ran back outside just in time to get in line with the other kids. Fifty cents! I could buy almost anything on the long list of pictured choices on the side of the truck. It was a good day.

I settled on a Drumstick˙ with fudge in the middle and flipped the other quarter into my pocket. As I sat under the big shade tree, enjoying my ice cream, something hit me in my gut like a punch from a playground bully. *Use my inside voice?* I knew what my grandmother meant, but all I could think about now were the nagging, incessant words in my head that constantly told me I was worthless. It was habitual now. Every time I felt like I let someone down, I felt worthless. When I couldn't make people around me happy, I felt worthless. But something was happening. The thoughts in my head were becoming more frequent, harder to overcome. I hated my inside voice.

Have you struggled with hating yours? For most of us who have endured trauma, especially as a child, we want to silence that voice. But you can't trust silence to be the thing to bring peace. It only brings quiet, which is not the same thing. You can find the courage to face that inner narrative. Stay with me, and we will get there.

My mom wound up marrying the man with the million-dollar smile and the cool sideburns. His name is Max White, and a few months after the wedding, he adopted my sister and me. We lived in a small rental house in a lower-income part of my hometown. We didn't have a lot, but we were together and happy, for the most part.

One of our neighbors was a strange man who sat on his front porch just watching people pass by. I am not sure if it was true, but the story circulating through the neighborhood was that he had suffered a mental breakdown after being in an accident that killed some children. Every day, as I walked past his house after school, he called me over to his porch and challenged me to spell the word *chrysanthemum* (I later learned those were the flowers that surrounded the porch where he sat). One day, he introduced me to a friend of his in the neighborhood. The man wore a ball cap with the letter C on the front of it. He stood very close to me when he talked to me, and I could smell stale alcohol and cigarettes on his breath, just like my biological father. I didn't think anything else about him, but we would soon cross paths again.

One of my friends had a large shed in his backyard. We were exploring it one day and accidentally found his older brother's stash of adult magazines. It felt exciting and scary to look at these forbidden images with my friend, but one day the porch man's scary friend came in and started looking along with us, as if we were all buddies. After that, he started running into me in the neighborhood more often than could be coincidental. He talked about the magazines and said things I didn't understand. Then one day, he told me to come over to his house a few blocks away because he wanted to show me something. This led to three years of sexual abuse at the hands of this man. He had me come over after school, gave me snacks, and then forced me to re-enact the pornographic scenes from the adult magazines and movies that littered his living room.

I know what some of you are thinking. *Why didn't you tell someone? Why did you continue to go to that man's house? Why weren't your parents watching you better?* First, most children freely roamed the neighborhood on their bikes. Like a lot of small-town kids, we just had to be home before the streetlights came on. As for why I didn't say something to someone, that one is easy: I was already a worthless enough burden, at least in my thoughts. I didn't want to cause any trouble for anyone, nor test whether anyone would bother coming to my rescue.

My newlywed parents were working hard to create a family. Max had instantly become a father of two children, ages six and one, and had a lot to learn about the role. I constantly felt like a burden, and I blamed myself for every struggle or bad thing that happened. My new dad was born with lung problems, so he had pneumonia a lot. One time, he had to be rushed to the hospital and was close to dying. I blamed myself for not being able to make him better. My dad's family struggled to accept my mom and sister and me at first. They worried about their young son becoming a father of two overnight. I blamed myself for that family struggle as well. Once, we were at a fish fry with my dad's family and an uncle, three sheets in the wind drunk, walked up to me, and said, "You're a worthless piece of sh** and will never deserve to be a White." I guess he wasn't happy that Dad had adopted me and given me his name. Did I tell anyone about this? No, of course I did not. Because I believed him. All I could do was stand there wondering how he had found out the truth about me.

The feelings of worthlessness had morphed into something much deeper. I even noticed the change in my dialogue. My inner voice had always made me *feel* worthless, but now I was saying the words: *I am worthless.* The feeling was damaging enough, but the words became an identity. My own words had hacked who I believed I was. Like a virus invades a computer and takes over the hard drive, this broken, painful narrative had overtaken my internal belief system. Rather than struggling with feelings, I now just resigned myself to my new identity of being a worthless and unlovable person. It hurt, but to my young mind, it made sense of things, so I didn't have to fight it anymore. I was so tired of fighting it.

Take heart. I know some of you read that last statement, and it hit a little too close to home. Don't give up the fight. If it seems too overwhelming, that's because it's too much for any one person to handle. So, do *now* what it took me forty years to do: ask for help. Someone who loves you will want to respond.

I did a very good job of wearing a smile on the outside and trying to make everyone around me happy, but on the inside, I was existing in a constant state of fear, shame, and chaos. I am sure some of you can relate. My path has crossed so many people that go about life polishing that perfect outer facade while slowly dying inside. Do you know the feeling of putting on that smile while the pain eats away at you? Maybe you believe the same lies I did. *No one cares about my problems. If I ask for help, others will see me as weak and broken. I must be the only one that struggles like this, so no one will understand.*

If you can identify with any of that, you are the reason I am writing this book and sharing my own story. I know from personal experience how hard it is to recover our identity once our own words hack us. It is hard, but it is not impossible. It doesn't have to take you forty years to get free, as it did me.

So, how do you go about mastering this process of discovery? First, know this: we all have that voice or narrative inside of us. Many of us just struggle with hearing it. We easily recall the good things and the positive experiences, but most of us bury those experiences where fear, shame, and trauma were born. In working with clients, we begin with the big question, "What do you fear most in life?" It may take a little time, but it usually rises to the surface. Taking that answer (in my case: I am worthless and unlovable), you begin to recall all the times you remember feeling that. Then, as you awaken those memories, you ask yourself a second question: *what was I saying to myself at that moment?* It can be challenging to bring unconscious memories into consciousness but stick with it. The good news is that our brain writes every moment of our story into our memories. It is not fun to recall painful things in our past like trauma and abuse but understanding the story we told ourselves in those moments will help us make sense of the mental, emotional, and relational struggles we may endure in our present.

After working through this process of discovery and raising awareness of the presence of your internal narrative, you now need to make sense of the power this damaged belief system has in your daily life. If fear is something we try to avoid talking about, the next inner demon is one we enjoy talking about even less. Meet fear's cousin: shame.

Embracing Light

- Do not fear awakening the painful parts of your narrative. Some of the greatest life lessons come from the deepest hurts.

- What do you fear most in life? Discovering and understanding the answer to this question can unlock a lot about those day-to-day surface struggles you may deal with.

- Words create worlds. The words you speak within yourself tend to create or influence the world you exist in. The good news: If your words support an environment of pain and chaos, then you can work to master a narrative that supports joy and peace.

- Listen to your narrative for any negative inner "I am" statements. They almost always point to the work you need to embrace to better value yourself and support a healthy belief system.

- Do not fear your fears. They are most often pointing to areas of unresolved trauma or pain. One of our greatest fears is the unknown, so confronting (making known) your fear narrative is your best first step in defeating it.

2

DISCLOSE

The Power of Narrative

Fear is the path to the dark side. Fear leads to anger.
Anger leads to hate. Hate leads to suffering.
—Yoda

I was working through my sexual abuse past with a therapist in Minnesota. As we journeyed from the events of the abuse into the addictions and struggles I had early in life, he asked me a question that caught me off guard.

"Have you struggled with hate through all of this, and if so, who would be on that list?"

I began thinking of all the characters throughout the chapters of my story, and tears began streaming down my face.

Looking at me with caring eyes, he said, "Is the list that long?"

"No, it is not long at all," I said, trying to smile through what was now full-on sobbing.

He told me I did not have to share if I wasn't ready. I was ready, but I did not know what to do with the answer. I stared him straight in the eyes, fully expecting him to call a foul on the answer I was about to give him.

"I have only ever hated one person in my life," I expressed with a fearful disdain.

"*Me.*"

I had struggled with hating myself ever since that day at the roadside park, and I continued with the same feeling right up to the moment of that conversation. He warned me that hate was a very destructive force that would overpower any system or person it possessed, especially if that hate was pervasive and long-lasting.

I knew my self-hate had done much damage in my own heart and mind, but I told him I would never allow it to hurt others around me. Six-year-old me had concluded it was my mission in life to make people happy and make them smile. He began to go back over the list we had created of life events that led me to his office. "Looks like a trail of hurt and pain to me," he observed. His response made me angry. I wasn't angry at him, but I was angry because he was right. The hate I experienced for myself had nurtured my fear, and it had helped to develop that hacked self-belief that I was a worthless and unlovable human. And now, it hit me like a ton of bricks that my pain had also hurt others. It was the last thing I ever wanted to happen.

Hate is a very common struggle for survivors of abuse. Please get help in working through that. Hate is not something you can contain without some form of damage and destruction to yourself and others. You deserve better.

The Power of Narrative

After we have raised awareness to that deep internal narrative, we all carry around, we need to make sense of how our story connects to and affects our daily lives; to disclose how this newfound narrative is present in our current, day to day struggles. I long avoided this process for three reasons: I felt powerless to face my past; I felt too worthless to share it with anyone else, and I had convinced myself it had no control over how I was living my life in the moment. Wow, how wrong I was on that last one.

I had dealt with a lot of internal struggles in life, most of which I kept private for fear of being seen as more worthless than I already felt. The major weapons in my daily mental-health struggles were deflection and avoidance. When I felt sad, I just worked harder to make more people happy, more people smile. When I felt anxious, I obsessed over the project or task I was currently involved in. When I was angry at myself, I got lost in loving and serving others.

Can you see the problem here? While I was working hard and experiencing great success at seeing to the needs of others, I was ignoring my own needs. When you feel worthless, self-care often feels like a very selfish act. In the many journeys I have shared while helping others through their own mental health and relationship struggles, I have learned this is very common, especially for survivors of childhood traumas.

I always saw avoidance and deflection as my only viable response to these internal struggles. I tried to face them, but to no avail. It was hard to understand why I was sad or why I felt so much anxiety. It was easy to see in the clients that I worked with. They brought very real-life issues with them that made their struggles make sense. I have nothing against the use of medication; I think it serves a purpose for some. But in my warped sense of self-worth, drugs were just another item on a long list that proved me broken and worthless. Instead of seeking help through therapy, medication, or even getting my basic emotional needs met, I decided that if I helped enough other people feel whole and happy, then someday my life would make sense. Can you identify? Let me say this loud and clear: Self-care is *never* selfish. It is necessary.

Thinking that helping others would fix me, of course, was a whimsical fantasy. I could help other people for the rest of my life and never be whole and at peace until I dealt with my own issues. When I was on that mountain in Tennessee, sitting on that boulder, I had a revelation. I saw the life I desired as a serene lake in the middle of a beautiful forest. The peace and joy it brought were all I wanted to feel on the inside. Sadness, anxiety, and this constant feeling of worthlessness were like ripples on the smooth surface of the lake. I saw the way I was trying to manage my own mental health journey as me rowing out in a boat trying to smooth out the ripples while ignoring the cause and source of them. Every time things got calm; more ripples came. The surface of the lake did not stay smooth. So, I spent years and years of my life trying to manage the ripples on the lake (my mind) by getting lost in helping others find their own peace. Train wrecks in life tend to wake you up. Avoidance of facing my needs had not only exacerbated my own pain and suffering, but now I faced a trail of hurt in those around me. Despite all the effort to help others, one truth remained: Hurt people, hurt people. I had to find a new way to deal with this.

Shame and Survival Brain

For much of my life, I struggled with something that was far more damaging than the sexual abuse and far more pervasive than anxiety, depression, and my lack of self-worth. I called it my monster or inner demon. I just knew it to be a force that would knock me to the ground when I least expected it. Sometimes all seemed right in life, my lake was calm and free of ripples.

Then, I could hear my inner monster. *Do you think you deserve to feel good about your life? You aren't smart enough to succeed at that job or project. These new people you are so excited about meeting are soon going to find you out. Remember, you are worthless and unlovable.*

The years of harboring my fears, holding them in the dark recesses of my mind, and not sharing them with anyone, had birthed this monster. That "inside voice" of mine had a name: *shame. Shame:* A painful feeling of humiliation or distress; an unpleasant, self-conscious emotion associated with a negative evaluation of self.[2]

Okay, I get that definition. But if that is shame, why isn't it something I only felt during my mental health struggles, the sexual abuse, or the times of my poor choices? Why was shame something that sucker-punched me during the good times in my life? Why was it something that forced me to hide my story from others?

The answer was a concept called survival brain. This is where we could go into a deep study of shame and the link to survival brain, citing a litany of professional journals and experts far smarter than I. But we will not go there in this story. Maybe that will be a future book. Suffice it to say that survival brain is a neurological response to trauma, an automatic process your brain uses to help you survive something unimaginable and overwhelmingly painful.[3] My experience was typical of many people's.

Trying to make sense of the pain and fear in the moment, many of us conclude that the horrible events must be our fault. That was what I did. I blamed the sexual abuse on myself. I must have deserved it, especially since it happened twice. But when you do what I did, and harbor the fear and shame for too long, it hacks the whole of your being. My belief system was turned upside down. On the outside, I created a facade of a happy, helpful man who loved life, but on the inside, I was fighting a constant battle with pain and chaos.

Living in this duality is part of what sustains survival brain. During trauma, such as being sexually abused, the brain goes into what we know as fight-or-flight mode. Things move very fast, and the normal "thinking" systems of our brain shut down and give way to simply surviving. When you cannot physically fight or flee, you emotionally disengage.[4] I remember that feeling. When my abuser coerced me into doing perverse things, I couldn't think. I lost all track of time and being. I was merely trying to breathe through the moment. After the abuse, I tried to make sense of things, to understand them. With my brain still reeling through fight-or-flight mode, and my thinking brain still on shutdown, I drew deeply erroneous conclusions about myself and who I was. I was just trying to understand what had happened. But some things just defy any form of making sense. Each time the abuse happened, I would go back to the thoughts that supported my new "hacked" identity of being worthless and deserving of what I was experiencing.

Many people that survive childhood trauma do what I did. We hold on to the experiences, hiding them away. We fear what others will think of us if we share. We don't want to be seen as damaged goods or labeled as mentally unstable. This is especially true of us men. We give in to the damaging social stigma that real men do not have struggles with mental health; they do not need to talk about trauma or painful things that happened a long time ago. That makes us weak. I mean, what real man talks about his feelings, right?

Let me say this loudly so everyone will hear: This is *the* most destructive thing we can do as men. When we hide our feelings, we deny ourselves the joy of intimacy with others, and we inevitably wind up hurting the people we most want to protect.

I know I am repeating myself, but one of the key things I learned in my journey that I love sharing with clients (and anyone that will listen, for that matter) is this: trauma is less about what we experience than about the narrative we write about the experience. The trauma ended for me. There was a time I was no longer being sexually abused. But the narrative of trauma stayed with me for forty years. That narrative nurtured and sustained the monster named shame. The broken narrative I believed about myself got me stuck in survival brain mode. I lived on a roller coaster ride between calm and chaos. Every time something good happened, shame sucker-punched me and reminded me I was wired for chaos and was not worthy of peace or joy.

The survival brain only operates in that one mode, fight, or flight. It does not do well at thinking and problem solving, nor does it thrive in peace and calm. A lot of survivors of trauma get stuck in this mode. You would think someone that has experienced the painful past of trauma would embrace peace, calm, and normalcy in life. If you're a friend or loved one of someone with trauma, believe me when I tell you we want to enjoy peace and happiness. We really do. But, being steeped in the belief that our struggles and pain are what we deserve, we often self-sabotage. If there is no chaos, we will create it. For many years, I have known I deserved better, and I have known I had more value than I allowed myself to experience. I just didn't believe it.

The Anxiety of Knowing and Not Believing

It took me so long to notice that I could help others find peace and healing despite not enjoying the same myself. The wounds were deeper than the shame of feeling unworthy. It was more than my error of only trying to just fight the symptoms of my mental health journey. Examining my story helped me achieve a drone view of my life. From that high vantage, I could look down at that inner lake that represented my mind and my desire for peace and see the truth—the painful and raw truth.

Every time things were going well, and the surface of my lake was smooth—*Bam!* A rock would plunge into the water and create a splashing, rippling chaos. But who was throwing the rocks? Who was breaking up my peace and calm?

It was *me*. The same person I struggled with hating. The shame that was birthed in me as a child and the survival brain that helped me get through the crazy fight-or-flight experiences of my abuse didn't trust peace, didn't believe in the reality of calm.

As a person who believes in God and professes to have a relationship with Jesus, I *know* who I really am. I know I have value and worth, irrespective of what other people think of me. But, because of my past, I couldn't believe this for most of my life. I felt God let me in with an asterisk next to my name, and I had to clean up the mess that I had allowed my past to create before enjoying the fullness of His love. I accepted my fear, shame, and anxiety because I "trusted" that this was my best self, what I deserved in life. Peace, calm, and love for myself was something I feared because I believed it would leave me as soon as I began to enjoy it. I also believed it was something only others were worthy of. As I moved through life, one experience after another entrenched my broken, hacked belief system.

I want to share a few of them for two reasons: I want you to see how damaging a hacked narrative can become if left alone or avoided, and I hope you can see yourself in some of these examples and awaken to your own story. I hunger to see people avoid the anxiety that comes with this dichotomous struggle between knowing and not believing.

One of my favorite things to do in the third grade was to play kickball at recess. I was good at it, and it gave me a sense of belonging. One day, I was picked last for a team. This didn't often happen since I was fast and could kick the ball a country mile. It wasn't the end of the world, but here is what my inner narrative said, *you were right for picking me last. How did you know how worthless I was? Probably because I am poor and don't have nice clothes. Maybe you even know what that man in my neighborhood is doing to me. I would pick me last, too, if I were you.*

In the fourth grade, I was standing on the playground alone, looking for someone to play with, when a large rock struck me in the throat. A student was just picking up rocks and seeing how far he could throw them; he wasn't intentionally throwing the rock at me. It was still a terrifying and painful experience. My first thought wasn't that it was dangerous, and the boy shouldn't be doing it. I thought I deserved it. *Who am I to think that anyone wants to play with me today?*

In the '90s, I had the highest-paying job I have had to date. It was a fun job in the advertising field, and my nearest boss was halfway across the country in Los Angeles. It was a dream job. Things were going great, and my territory had expanded to twenty-six counties. *Bam!* There it was, that rock in my lake, ripples upsetting my calm, peaceful waters. The voice reminded me I did not deserve this success; I was worthless and would surely fail. Three months later, I quit.

I was dating a nice young woman in college (before meeting my precious wife). She treated me perfectly and brought out the good in me. But, as I had done in two other relationships, I struggled with feeling like I didn't deserve the love my heart desired. The rock in the lake this time was lying. I was self-sabotaging, and I got caught, and she broke off the relationship. I was devastated. My shame-filled mind told me I deserved it. I broke a mirror on my car door and began slashing at my wrist. With each cut, I was yelling at myself in anger, "You are a worthless piece of sh**! You can't do anything right!"

Thankfully, I didn't fatally hurt myself (one thing I'm glad not to have done right). I have always believed I didn't really want to end my life then. Rather, I could no longer stomach the incessant ripples in the lake of my peace and calm. I couldn't handle my inside voice anymore. The anxiety was getting to be too much. It was many years after this that I reached the healing journey I share here, but God soon brought me the woman that would be my wife, and she gloriously stood in the gap with me until that day came. You will learn more about her later.

I know this line of thinking may seem crazy to some. I almost get it when I hear people say, "Just get over it," or "Stop dwelling on the past," but it simply isn't that easy. The brain is equally powerful when it is operating the way it was meant to, and when it's hacked by destructive and painful beliefs. Once shame has taken hold, things deteriorate. You make illogical leaps from negative events to self-blame. One rare, bad moment becomes the defining event of your life. You destroy the good things that happen to you rather than wait for them inevitably to fail you, as you believe they will.

For years, it was hard for me to trust myself. I doubted every decision I made. I worried about whether I was enough for everyone around me, whether I was making their life better or worse with my presence.

After you have raised awareness of this story that you mentally write about your experiences, you can begin to see how pervasive and destructive unresolved, painful narratives have been in your life. Now, it is time to become very real with yourself. Where you find yourself in life at this very moment has much to do with the freedom or bondage that your inner narrative has created. Your internal dialogue will always determine your external direction.

EMBRACING LIGHT

- Hate is not something you can hold on to without some level of pain or damage. It will invade every area of your life. If you deal with hate from past trauma, seek help with processing it through.

- If you struggle with anxiety or other mental health issues, be brave and look behind the curtain. You may find destructive internal narratives from your past creating or exacerbating those struggles. Getting to the root of the issue could help free you in ways you never thought possible.

- Self-care is imperative to have the strength to master a healthy internal narrative. Get an accountability partner to help keep you moving forward.

- Shame and destructive negative self-evaluation may mean you are stuck in survival mode, especially if you have past unresolved trauma. Get professional help from a counselor or life coach who has been trained in trauma recovery.

- Knowing something rarely sparks positive action and growth. It takes belief to create the movement necessary to live a life of balance, peace, and joy.

3

DECIPHER

The Prison of Narrative

*I will love the light for it shows me the way,
yet I will endure the darkness because it shows me the stars.*
—*Og Mandino*

You will never meet another family of bigger nature lovers than us. Most people will avoid hitting squirrels or puppies when driving down the road, but my wife will dodge caterpillars and beetles if she sees them in time. I mean, we really love animals and nature. Because of that love, we are sad when we find dead little frogs or turtles in our pool because they could not get back out once they fell in. We finally found some fake lily pads to put in the pool to give them a place to rest until we could catch them with the net and release them.

We have a pond in our backyard, so they often find their way to the pool, thinking it is the same environment. Sure, it is water, but unlike the pond, there is no way to get out once they fall in. The only way these little creatures can survive is to get into the net that I offer them so that I can release them back into their natural habitat. But what do they do when

29

they see me put that net in the water? They swim away from me. They dive into the deep end, trying to escape the only real salvation available.

After one rainy night, I was trying to rescue four frogs that had all found their way to the pool. They scurried everywhere but into the net. I was frustrated. It was hot, and I had things to do. I yelled out, as if they could understand me, "Don't you want to be helped?"

Do you know how you get those deep life lessons when you least expect them? I could hear God speak to my heart. *Haven't you been like those frogs for much of your life? I have offered you help. I have put people in your path who love you and care for you. And what did you do? You ran away from the net and into the deep end of the pool, believing it was safer.*

Wow! Okay, God, I hear you. I guess He also had a hand in helping me name this chapter: decipher—meaning to put in understandable terms.

The Warden and the Prisoner

After the trauma of my sexual abuse, my world got progressively smaller. Not in any way that most people would notice, but inside myself, where it counted most. All the systems God hard wires us with (joy, peace, self-worth, love, patience, faith) were in chaos. It became hard to trust myself to know what was best for me. I put too little trust in deserving people and too much in undeserving ones. When things were going well, that destructive internal narrative shouted that I was worthless and unlovable. *Don't believe in yourself too much, Buddy, because things will never turn out the way you want them to. You can't be yourself with these people; they will hate you. Don't get your hopes up, because you know at some point the rug will be pulled out from under you.* Doesn't this all sound crazy? You would never believe this about someone else, so why would you believe it about yourself?

What I noticed on my own journey is something I have seen repeated in the countless trauma clients I have worked with: we experience the loss of that natural, internal, safe space we are all wired to have. The narrative of our core fear and shame builds a construct of limiting beliefs inside our minds. Think of it as a very dysfunctional, substitute safe place, like a blanket laced with barbed wire. When we are cold, we need that blanket. But it causes pain and damage. The problem is, it's the only blanket we have, and the only one we believe we deserve. Have you ever felt like you couldn't trust anything good for you or that could help you? I am pretty sure it's not just me. That is what limiting beliefs do. Think of your negative internal voice. What does it say to you? *You are not enough. You are a failure. You know they do not love you. Do you really think you can accomplish that project?* Every time we hear words like this and do not face and replace them with truth, we give them more power over us. Our negative self-beliefs, especially centered on the fear and shame of past trauma, are like walls that slowly close in on us. For me, that process happened over years. I didn't notice how much smaller my world was getting. I just woke up one day and realized I was living my life in a prison cell.

I didn't want to be worthless and unlovable, but I truly believed, for a long time, that I was. I believed in the painful limiting beliefs constantly swimming around my head more than I believed what God and those who loved me were telling me. That only means one thing. My resignation to live life from my prison cell was a choice. No one was forcing me to believe these lies. I was not still being abused. I wasn't hearing these damning words from anyone else but myself. I was a prisoner of my own making. My words were the architect of the prison, and my limiting beliefs were the warden.

If you have ever felt this way, first, here's a nice big ((hug)). You are going to be okay. Why do I know this? I was in my own prison for a long time. I decorated the walls and allowed myself to think it was the best I deserved. It became strangely comfortable. But I eventually found freedom. Second, remember this: words create worlds. If they have the power to imprison us, then they have the power to set us free. We will get there soon.

Pain Is My Friend?

No one enjoys feeling pain. We fear it. We run from it. We try to numb it. It is true that too much pain, whether it be physical, mental, or emotional, can, indeed, be dangerous. But what if we looked at pain differently? When it comes to the pain resulting from past trauma or negative experiences, what if we saw it as a source of freedom rather than the thing supporting the bondage and limiting beliefs? Stay with me here. Let's look at a physical example of what I am talking about. Say you have extreme and near-constant knee pain. What do most people do? They run from it; they medicate it away. Sometimes, especially in the case of us men, we may pretend it doesn't bother us. One thing many of us do, especially we Americans, is to go to the doctor and insist on a pill or a shot to end the pain and suffering immediately.

I get it. A painful knee can ruin an otherwise great day. But look at it this way: your knee hurts, so something is not right, and the nerves in your knee are sending signals to the brain. What is the better option? You listen to the pain. You go to a professional that can speak that pain's language and you embrace it with them. Rather than a quick fix, you hear what the pain and the professional are trying to tell you. You get X-rays and other tests, finally learning that you have a torn ligament in your knee. It is a simple surgery, but if you do not respond to the pain and get the knee fixed, things will keep getting worse. Pain is your friend. It just tries to tell you that something needs to be fixed.

It is the same situation with our mental health. We run from thoughts and feelings that bring us pain. We medicate them away, whether it be with drugs, addictions, or unhealthy habits. We do anything to not feel the pain. I am with you. Forty years of my life was spent running from, medicating, and trying to deny that pain caused by my dysfunctional internal narrative. I feared it. I thought I was powerless to overcome it. Fighting against the pain almost killed me—literally, through struggles with addiction and a suicide attempt—and it almost destroyed my heart from all the hurt I caused others along the way.

But, as I said earlier, train wrecks in life can wake you up. I finally did face down my pain. Do you know what I learned? It was less dangerous facing it than it was spending all my effort to avoid and deny it. And the biggest thing I learned was this: my pain, like in the knee pain example, was really my friend. It was trying to tell me something. My pain was trying to show me the unresolved parts of my story. It was trying to show me the way to freedom. It was hard, initially, to face it down. Like going to the doctor that speaks the pain language of a hurt knee, it just takes surrounding yourself with someone that speaks the pain language of trauma. Facing down your pain and fear is the first step in the journey to freedom.

Acceptance and Life's Toolbox

Every successful journey has one big thing in common: a good start. Being prepared and having the right frame of mind means all the difference in whether your journey will lead you to your desired destination. For those of us who have experienced trauma, that desired destination is freedom from fear, shame, and damaging, destructive internal narratives. I have started this journey countless times and found myself quitting early and not getting anywhere near the freedom I desired and deserved. Why did I quit early? I skipped a simple but essential step: acceptance.

While acceptance is a simple step, it is not an easy step. Acceptance, within the journey from bondage to freedom, looks like this:

- I have awakened to the whole of my past story, and I accept it.

- I understand the damage it caused and still causes me, and I accept it.

- I see how my broken internal narrative led to some poor life choices, and I accept them.

- I know my current path is unhealthy and needs changing, and I accept it.

Acceptance is *not*

- saying all those things that happened are okay; or

- saying you will stay stuck here forever.

Acceptance is about seeing the reality of where you are in the moment. It is about gathering all your resources, even if they are scarce, and developing a plan to move toward freedom. I remember this place on my journey. It was painful, but, in hindsight, I see it was necessary. Acceptance brings ownership, the kind of ownership that brings you to your knees. I was sitting in the office with a new friend that I had just met. We shared much of the same past stories: sexual abuse, addictions, poor choices, and living in complete bondage. He had experienced his healing journey about thirty years prior to our meeting. As he shared how he had failed to find freedom so many times, I asked him, "What made the difference the last time, the time that it all fell into place?" He responded, "I accepted the truth of my story: I had been sexually abused. I allowed myself to stay in secret bondage for too long. I made some very poor choices that brought much pain to me, as well as others that I held dear. It broke me. My reality brought brokenness, and ultimately, that brought freedom."

I did not like how closely his story mirrored mine, but his truth was my truth. Before I left my friend in Minnesota, I, too, embraced acceptance. I allowed brokenness to overtake me. I trusted this was a step of courage and strength rather than weakness, as I had believed my whole life. And he was right: It made all the difference in the world. It awakened me to my reality. Acceptance helped me to stop dwelling on the past. It gave me the courage to embrace the present, to embrace the starting point of my journey to freedom.

I remember this exercise of acceptance leading me to dream about a toolbox. I like to call it life's toolbox. It's the one God gives every one of us. It is full of all the shiny tools we need to experience joy and peace, faith, and hope, and to love and feel loved. But my toolbox was beaten and battered by my life of bondage. As I opened it, I saw what represented the reality of my present state of being. There were no pristine, God-given tools. There was only a broken hammer and a used roll of duct tape. No wonder I was doing such a rotten job building a healthy inner life. Someone had taken most of my tools and broke or used up what was left. I was going to need help to repair my toolbox and get some new tools.

Acceptance is hard. But every great journey requires a starting point, and this was mine.

Cowboy Boots, Yellow Raincoats, and Flipped Economies

The inner world of a trauma survivor, or anyone stuck in their own private mental health battle, is full of chaos and destruction. Those God-given systems that bring us peace and joy and a healthy sense of self are all offline. The hacked narrative

35

of broken self-beliefs brought on by the incessant feelings of fear, shame, and inadequacy leads us to a place of loneliness and mistrust. We can be in a peaceful setting, surrounded by people who love us, and at the same time, be hating ourselves for what is going on inside our heads. But even when I was at my lowest point, I still hungered for those God-given desires for belonging, love, and purpose. I hungered to feel safe, courageous, and wanted. I just did not feel I had the ability within me any longer to have those things. I was emotionally and mentally bankrupt.

In what I call flipped economies, many trauma survivors will begin to look on the outside for the fulfillment of those needs that should be filled from within. When we cannot derive value within ourselves, we will look for people and things in the world to satisfy that need. The first instance I can recall in my story was the fireflies. I was afraid of the dark. I was afraid of what I had sometimes experienced in the dark. Not being able to feel safe myself, I looked for the fireflies to protect me.

At around that same age, I started begging my mom for a pair of cowboy boots. Sure, you live in Texas, doesn't everyone wear cowboy boots at some point? But for me, it was much more. I lacked courage. Do you remember me saying I was afraid of everything? Well, at that point in my young life, the most courageous people I saw were on the westerns my family watched on television, and they all wore cowboy boots. So, mom got me a pair, and she could never get them off me. I wore them with shorts; I wore them with pajamas, and I even tried to wear them to bed.

When I started school, my grandfather bought me a bright yellow raincoat with matching boots and a hat. He said it was the same kind he wore while working on the railroad. It was heavy, thick, and hot. But there was something about it I could not get enough of. The weight of the raincoat pressed on my body like a big hug that I so hungered for.

So, I used the fireflies for safety, the cowboy boots for courage, and the raincoat for belonging. How do you think that worked out for me? Right, it didn't at all. They were cheap substitutes for what I was created to feel from within.

They didn't do me much good, but they also didn't do me any harm. As we grow up and those internal voices get louder and more incessant, many of us look to things far more destructive than dependence on raincoats or cowboy boots. I first tried alcohol at fifteen. That isn't too rare in our small town in East Texas, but from the beginning, alcohol, for me, was something much more than a Friday night recreation with friends. I noticed that it quieted the monster's voice; it made me feel like I belonged and as if the people around me really cared for me. Soon after, I experienced marijuana. It took me to new places of freedom from the voices, the lack of self-belief, and the feeling of worthlessness. I liked who I was with alcohol and weed. I was what I would call a high-functioning user. I went through three years of high school and four years of college with good grades, despite spending a massive amount of that time under the influence of substances. Halfway through this period of my life, I discovered the drug Ecstasy. It further enhanced my euphoric feeling of being demon-free inside my head. I know, whether you have had this experience or not, you see the flaw already.

Being under the influence of those drugs never helped me find my true self. It only hid, temporarily, my painful, true reality. Besides the damaging and destructive possibilities of my drug use, I knew they were just like the cowboy boots and the raincoat, a cheap substitute for what I was really created to experience. In 1984, the painful reality of looking for things, people, and experiences to complete me rocked my world. Within six months, I had two life-awakening accidents. I had a major car wreck—while under the influence—that should have killed people. I also probably should have gone to jail, but the people I hit showed me a heap of unwarranted grace.

Later that year, I fell from an upper-story window of my fraternity house while under the influence again. It could have killed me as well. I was on a destructive course, and I didn't know what was going to kill me first; my inner chaos or the chaos I created with my poor choices.

I hated who I was on the inside, and I was beginning to hate who I was on the outside. For much of my life, the only peace and calm I felt was temporarily manufactured by my efforts to please and impress people, or when I drowned out the voices with substances. Most of that changed when I met my wife. I would like to say it all changed, but it didn't. Like everyone else in my life, I hid the most painful parts of my story from her for a long time. She has only known about my sexual abuse experience for eleven years. I assumed, as I did with my dad, that if she knew my dark past and the demons I carried around, she would leave me.

Early in our marriage, I still struggled a little with alcohol. Once we got a handle on that, I became an angry person. It hurt that I could not help her understand, but at the time, I did not know what I was angry about either. Even though our life was amazing and filled with love, she could not help me overcome the battle with my inner demons. For one thing, I did not let her know the whole story, and second, it was not her place to heal me. All she could do was love me through it. Although I made it very hard for her at times, she never gave up on me.

For a lot of our marriage, I defeated one struggle by falling into another one. When alcohol was no longer an issue, I drowned out the inner voices with a porn addiction. This was a very familiar world for me, having been exposed to it so pervasively by my second abuser. I overcame that struggle by going back to the thing that six-year-old me chose as his life goal: to make people happy and make them smile. On the day I met the man that would become my father, I decided if I could not save myself, I would save the world. Hmm, six-year-old little boys can dream big, can't they? I became obsessed with helping people in need. Yes, most of the motivation in serving the needs of others came from my faith in God and His call to love one another. But I would be remiss if I did not acknowledge that it also served the purpose of drowning out the negative internal voices. The only problem was, much like the drugs, it only drowned out the pain while I was in the act of serving. And there was never such a thing as enough.

I had put myself in a very dangerous position. In psychology, that feeling that it is your job to save the world is called a messiah complex. I felt I couldn't defeat my inner demons, and alcohol, drugs, and porn were too destructive, so I did just enough good for others to keep the voices of worthlessness at bay. God used my efforts over twenty years to help a lot of people. He spoke through a jackass, so I guess He could use my works despite my misaligned motivations.

I have had a lot of friends question why I chose to share the part of my story you are about to hear. I could easily leave it out, and everything would still make sense. But I want you to see the weight of our choices and the damage they can do when we rely on external things to try to satisfy internal needs. A statement I shared here earlier, and that I spoke to myself many years ago, would come back to haunt me: "If I cannot help myself, I will help enough other people, and that will someday lead me to the freedom I hunger for."

All my life, I loved people intensely. It was born out of the hatred for myself and the feeling that I was unlovable because of the abuse I endured. I learned a lot of childhood sexual abuse survivors often overcompensate in their love for others. It has always been like I was trying to out-love my internal hate. The greater the need people had around me, the harder I pressed in to love them and meet their needs. The strange thing is, that led to the event in my story which almost destroyed me, while at the same time becoming the

39

impetus for pressing me into the freedom and healing journey that I had been chasing for forty years.

What happened? I met *that* person, *the* one who, by helping, I could finally set myself free from my own struggles. Save this person and I would finally save myself. Why did I choose this one person over all the others? Part of it is a mystery to me, to be honest, but I think a big part of it was this person shared a story very similar to my childhood experiences. Her story is not mine to tell, but it had enough similarities that something made me think helping her find freedom would free me as well. That process became too personal, too intimate—because it meant more than it ever should have—and that eventually led to an affair.

Hurt people, hurt people. I hate that statement. I hate how true it is, and I hate hurting people. It broke my heart that my failure to find freedom from my past before now had led to this. I had allowed my internal brokenness to lead me to something far worse than alcohol, drugs, or porn. I had betrayed trust, let people down, and hurt the people most dear to me—my wife and kids.

It was a dark time for all of us. I could have stayed stuck right there—it almost happened. I could have ended it all—I thought long and hard about it. I spent all my life helping others, so it was too much to bear that I had hurt people. From the moment it happened, it became part of my story, and as much as I wanted to, I could not rewind time. I could only do what I did: accept the place of brokenness I was at, give my failure, brokenness, and weakness to God, and work to do better. All that could redeem my poor choice was God, and He did that the moment I gave it to him. In my moment of greatest brokenness, I felt myself moving forward into freedom and healing. I vowed then that I would give God my story so it might help others avoid the failures I endured.

Besides all the pain, it was also a watershed moment of change in my life. I hesitate to say it is what I needed to happen, but my wife would tell you she believes it. I was steeped in the grief of my past for so long, so entrenched in the belief that I was worthless and unlovable, that I was only going to move forward when my world was turned completely upside down. This poor choice broke me. It brought me to the end of myself. There isn't a day that goes by that I don't wish I could have reached that moment of clarity without hurting so many people so badly. I owe everything in my life to the grace shown to me by God, my wife, and my family. We took a mistake that was meant for destruction and turned it into the action plan we needed. I would have chosen any other event but this one, but it became a chapter in my story, and all we can do is embrace our story and learn from every piece of it.

You have raised awareness to your internal narrative. You have acknowledged how your hacked self-beliefs cause pain and chaos in your daily life. You have worked to understand and make sense of the prison of bondage that unresolved trauma can become. Now, we switch gears. Now, we recognize the potential our narrative can hold to bring us to freedom. Every bad experience, every poor choice, and every moment of pain hold the potential to teach us and move us forward. Our stories will either write us or we will write our stories. Let us use our words to dismantle the prison of limiting beliefs and lay the foundation for freedom and healing. You deserve this.

Embracing Light

- Do not be like the frog in the pool. Be aware of your surroundings. Things you avoid or give little thought to may be there to provide you with forward movement on the path you desire.

- Sometimes, our safe spaces are not the best spaces for us. Listen for statements in your internal narrative that are negative, lacking in hope, and keeping you in a box. You may be supporting your own bondage.

- Do not be too quick to avoid or medicate away your pain. It is often trying to tell you that something needs your attention. You may not like it. It may be uncomfortable at first. But listening to your pain may lead you out of a place of bondage and into freedom.

- Acceptance is not saying that everything is okay the way it is. It is also not saying that what happened in the past is okay. The act of acceptance is the conscious act of acknowledging the reality of where you are in the present moment. It is an imperative step for the start of any successful journey.

- You have value because you are *you*. The phrase "You are enough" is not just some catchy phrase for a meme or a coffee cup. It is the truth. Be careful not to look to the outside world to fulfill your intrinsic needs such as joy, peace, and self-worth.

4

DISMANTLE

The Potential of Narrative

Start where you are. Use what you have. Do what you can.
—Arthur Ashe

Spring of 2010 held so much promise. Our son was a senior in high school and excited about graduating. He had recently been selected All-East-Texas and All-State after a banner year of soccer saw the team rally to finish second in the state. After spending a month in a wheelchair following major reconstructive surgery on my calves, I was finally up and moving again. The recovery was rough, but not nearly as bad as the debilitating pain I had suffered for almost fifteen years. All in all, life was good.

We were having our customary Sunday dinner at my parents' house when the phone rang. Mom got up to answer it as she said, "Who the heck is calling us on a Sunday afternoon while I'm trying to enjoy dinner with family?" After saying hello, she stood there silently listening to the caller. Her face went white, and she fell back against the wall and slid down to the floor as she dropped the phone.

"Betty?" Dad asked. "Who was it? What did they say?"

Her voice trembled as if the weight of the world had just fallen on her. "It's cancer," she said. "Your tests came back, and they said it was cancer."

We all jumped up from the table, crying frantically as my dad helped my mother up from the floor. A million questions flew out of our mouths at once. We did not even know that my father had any issues that required a test. My parents told us they were waiting until they knew everything before sharing it with us.

We couldn't stop crying, doubting, and trying to wrap our heads around the gravity of the news that phone call had injected into our peaceful and happy Sunday afternoon. All of us were crying and frantic, except my dad. He stood at the kitchen counter looking stoic and resolved, almost peaceful. I was a basket case. This was my dad, my friend, my mentor, and my fishing buddy.

"How can you look so calm?" I asked him, with an air of frustration in my voice.

He looked at all of us and exclaimed, "What are you going to do? It is what it is."

In the moment, I did not like his answer at all. I thought my dad was being flippant or too accepting during this deep life crisis. But it would soon come to represent a major life lesson for us all. I proudly used to say that my dad had a high school diploma and a Ph.D. in life. He was constantly teaching us meaningful life wisdom with the simplest of words. Life got hectic fast as Mom and Dad met with doctors to determine a strategy for the battle ahead. It was hectic, but things never got too crazy to skip going fishing.

Dad and I were enjoying an afternoon on our favorite pond and as much as I resisted, I couldn't help but bring up the topic of cancer. He looked at me in the back of the boat, and with a smile, he said, "Boy, don't mess up a good day of fishing talking about bad news." Okay, fair enough. So, I asked him about those words: It is what it is.

Here is his beautiful explanation: "I could cry. I could wonder what I did to deserve this. I could hate myself for not quitting chewing tobacco sooner or working in that factory in the '70s that handled asbestos. I could question everything about my past and fear everything in my future, but what will that get me? Declaring, "It is what it is" helps me be in the moment. Don't you always tell people to embrace their moments? Well, that's what I am doing. It helps me focus on the things I can control, the real things right in front of me. It helps me bring all my energy, physical, mental, emotional, and spiritual, together to help me in this fight for my life. More than anything, it helps me to just keep living and not let cancer define me."

That statement taught me one more lesson I would have rather not learned. No one knows the future, and we didn't know what Dad's cancer battle would look like. It was six months. Four of those months were brutal and filled with chemo and surgeries, but for two of them, he felt well enough to go fishing and build a couple of more wheelchair ramps for those in need. He lived life on his own terms. Cancer didn't define him in his last days. He helped us to see that success in life is not about what the end of the journey looks like, it's about how you lived each moment on the journey. He was taken from us far too soon, but his life was full of joy, love, and peace. It is what it is.

Those five words have a lot to do with me getting to this point in my own journey of freedom and healing. In those words, I embraced the courage to be vulnerable with my story. I discovered what it was like to be fully present with myself. I found the strength to ask for help. Thank you, Dad.

When all hope seems lost and you cannot find your way out of the darkness, stop what you are doing and take a deep breath. Pull your thoughts into the present. Let go of the worries of the past and the unknowns of the future, and say to yourself, "It is what it is." Now, hold on to what you can control and plan your next best step only. Then, after you have made that step, repeat.

Speak Your Truth. It is the Light in Your Darkness

When I was a kid, I loved spending the night with my Mam-maw and Pap-paw. They lived in a huge, old country house on eighteen acres. I could explore, play with the farm animals, and go fishing to my heart's content. But at night, living out in the country, a lot of scary sounds started up that we didn't get in our little hometown. As I said, I feared everything as a kid.

When I stayed the night, I slept in a large bedroom on the opposite side of the house from my grandparents. There was a large floor-to-ceiling window right next to my bed. When the sky was clear, you could fall asleep watching the stars and moon go by. One night, my attention was drawn to something that terrified me. It looked as if a very large man was standing at the top of the hill with one arm outstretched. There was also a loud, incessant thumping noise coming from the same direction. What did he want? Why didn't he move? I convinced myself that it was a monster, and after that, I no longer wanted to spend the night at my grandparents' house. I would refuse every offer.

My dad, wanting to get to the bottom of things, finally asked me why I had such a change of heart. I was reluctant to tell him, even afraid to tell him for fear he would think I was cowardly (i.e., worthless). I finally described the large man and the loud noise. He went to the bedroom to investigate. He looked out the window and then looked at me as he cracked a smile. He said, "Come with me, boy. We are going for a dune buggy ride." I never turned that down.

We went out of the driveway and into the pasture of the neighbor's house. As he topped the hill, he stopped the dune buggy next to a large dead tree. "Does anything look familiar?" he asked. Nothing stood out to me. He told me to turn and look down the hill to my right. "What do you see?" he asked with a smile. It was my grandparents' house. He positioned me between the house and the big dead tree and asked me to listen. I could hear crows, cows, and then the loud thumping noise that the large man had been making. He pointed across the pasture at an oil derrick moving up and down like a slow-motion bucking bronc. "There is your loud thumping noise. You just never paid attention to it during the daylight." I always thought my dad was a genius. He then outlined the dead tree with his finger and said, "Kind of looks like a large man with an outstretched arm, doesn't it?" But you had probably guessed that already.

What is the point of this little story? Sometimes, you just need to speak truth into your darkness. Truth is light, and it reveals the lies that the darkness protects. This is the same for unprocessed trauma, fears we cannot shake, and shame we are enslaved by. These things are darkness; we aren't meant for them. We avoid them because we fear things we cannot control or things we do not understand. Sometimes, just bringing them into the light begins a healing process. Speaking the truth of our story, while painful, connects us to our potential to find freedom. It sounds easy; I know. But talking about things like fear, shame, and the pain of past trauma is hard in today's world.

We are a culture that holds the connection to millions in the palm of our hands, while people walk around us lonely and hurting. This digital leash lulls us into a world where everyone is perfect; no one has any problems and asking for help appears as a weakness or at least a buzzkill. I am not saying it is the whole world's fault for someone going through pain alone, but we have a crisis in the stigma this culture has nurtured by equating the acknowledgment of struggle with mental health issues as weakness or brokenness.

I once asked a friend what he thought the most spoken word in church on Sunday morning was. He gave the obvious answers of Jesus or grace. I challenged him to consider that the correct answer might be fine, or good, or any other similar words that exclaim that life is perfect and free of struggle. This is not a bash on church culture. I am a Christian and a Jesus follower, but I just see this as reality. You can hear it in the hallways and in the small groups gathered around Bible study. "How are you today, Bill?" "Oh, we are doing great, everything is perfect." I have met too many "Bills" that said some version of this on Sunday morning while their life was falling apart, or their marriage was in shambles. We need to learn to connect to those around us better, to listen more attentively, and to break the stigma that mental, emotional, or relational health struggles are a sign of failure or weakness. Some well-meaning people have told me that Sunday morning is not the time to be sharing your struggles with others. I say, when is there a better time than when we're gathered to worship the one whose strength is made perfect in our weakness? Who, if not our fellow Christians, should we expect to receive our struggles?

Breaking that stigma must begin with us. We must take responsibility to embrace our story and, once we understand our narrative and how it has us in bondage, be humble and vulnerable to share it with someone. Speaking the truth of the darkness in our story brings us light. It is life-giving light, and even though the process can be painful, it is a healing pain that draws us out of bondage and into freedom. Have you spoken about your pain or darkness with others? If not, find the courage to find a professional or a friend that won't judge and embrace that story with them. Remember my friend in the coffee shop? He helped me to see my inner light. Sharing with him did not fix everything, but it set me on the path of belief, freedom, and healing.

Will the Real Trauma Please Stand Up?

I have met so many people that tried to battle their trauma, to wrestle with the monsters from their past, and they were exhausted, beaten down to believe the prison created by their trauma and the hopelessness they often felt were just their cross to bear in life. I can identify with them all too well. I was in a constant state of chaos fatigue for much of my life. It took everything I had to keep the monsters of my past at bay with one hand while working to create a life of smiles, joy, and being everything that I thought others needed me to be with the other.

It's important to recognize that I have felt real joy with my wife, children, and friends, and I have known real career and social success. Being broken does not mean nothing in your life is going well. But for those of us in the bondage of past trauma, any good comes at the price of anxiety, stress, depression, and the constant expectation that all those good things will be taken from us at any moment. It is like playing tug-of-war with yourself. You can't win without losing.

Trying to battle something that has already happened truly is futile. Therefore, understanding the true power of trauma comes more from the narrative, or story, we write about that experience rather than the event itself. It awakens us to where our fight for freedom should be focused. Our narrative is present with us. The lies and limiting beliefs that hold us in bondage in that prison are something more tangible that we can wrestle with. Words create worlds.

I spent all my life running and hiding from the experiences of my past, when the real battle was with the story I was living in my mind. My fear and shame created that prison, and my words were like a bungee cord, reminding me of my worthlessness. I ventured out in life, enjoying my moments, and loving those around me, but one thought or feeling could snap me back into that prison and remind me of who I really was. When I grew tired of trying to battle that internal shame, I tried to engage my anxiety. But working on my anxiety without confronting the narrative that fueled it was like putting a band-aid on a bleeding artery. I have met a good number of clients that came to me just looking for a better band-aid because they feared facing the reality of their internal narratives. If you struggle with anxiety, depression, or feelings of worthlessness, I am not saying they do not deserve attention. I am saying to be truly free; you must look at your internal narrative and how it might support or exacerbate those struggles. Embrace the real you. Embrace your full story. Every part of it has the power to bring redemption, freedom, and light into your life. The journey is never perfect, but it is beautiful.

The Perfection Paradox

Since all our lives look so perfect on social media, that must mean perfection is and should be the goal, right? The perfect life. The perfect marriage. The perfect career. A life that is truly "gram-worthy."

If you haven't heard the news yet, I'm here to tell you now: it is all a myth and a dangerous myth at that. I am not saying we should not strive to live good lives that make for lovely pictures and even better memories, but we shouldn't do it so the whole of our success is measured by whether we can attain the perfection we chase. Trauma survivors are often the world's worst at this. Or is it just me? I was so accustomed to my assumption that everyone would eventually discover my past and declare me worthless and unlovable that it led me to believe I must be perfect or nothing at all. I quit jobs and abandoned great projects when I felt those feelings of failure coming on. In doing so, I led myself to fear mistakes and fear my past failures. This prevented me from learning, changing, and growing.

Embrace your imperfections. They are stones on the foot-path toward growth. You are not your flaws, mistakes, or pain, but you may have grown because of them. You are you, imperfect you. Strive to be a better version of who you were yesterday rather than demanding perfection.

Monsters, Triggers, and Facades

Everyone I have ever worked with through past trauma or painful experiences describes that battle with internal monsters or demons. Where do they come from? Why do we feel powerless to defeat them? My monster was first created to be a scapegoat for all the pain of sexual abuse. It was someone that I could blame things on, that I could scream out to. When we go into survival mode during the experience of trauma, our mind tries to make sense of things. But we do not do a very good job of that while in the fight-or-flight mode.

My monster put up walls to "protect" me. I use air quotes as I say the word *protect,* because that protection came at the cost of bondage. You see, the monster protected me by sup-porting what I believed about myself. It is like he was saying, "Okay, I know you feel worthless and unlovable and that makes the outside world a scary place. So, I will help build a safe place for you and we will hide it with a facade to make people think you are doing great. That way, you won't have to face them; you won't have to deal with your fear and shame. Just accept it; I've got you."

If you have never dealt with trauma, I know that sounds crazy. But I know a good number of you are thinking, how did he get in my head? That is exactly what my monster did. He made me believe that accepting my fear, shame, and pain was my best self.

The monster was also the one doing the gut-punching I mentioned earlier. When things were going well and I felt like maybe I could live with more joy and freedom, the monster roared out the reminder that I was worthless and unlovable, and the world was a place to be feared. That may sound like a contradiction but notice the common thread: the monster was the center of truth. He decided what was safe and unsafe; he held the reins to my life.

But guess what I learned? When I started battling the limiting beliefs of my internal narrative, something sounded familiar—the monster's voice and the way he spoke to me. It was *me. I* was the monster! *I* created him. This was huge. If my words created my internal monster, couldn't my words destroy him, too?

The answer is *yes.* But making this happen is not so easy. The monster operates in the darkness, so he hates the light. The monster is only needed when there is chaos and pain, so he hates peace and joy. He hates the truth, and he is not needed once you discover the true you. So, if you are still battling the internal monster born out of your trauma, smile at him. Let him see you smile, and you tell him, "I created you, and I am about to dismantle you. You are no longer needed here."

I often work with clients that are beaten and battered by incessant triggers stirring up the pain of their past trauma and the anxiety that accompanies it. They all describe the same feelings of hopelessness and lack of control. They painfully share the feeling of the elephant on their chest and the racing thoughts in their heads, like a hamster spinning out of control on his wheel. But what if you could gain control of your triggers? What if you discovered you already have the power to control them? Guess what; you do. We all do. I used to be in complete bondage to triggers. A person said something, and I felt worthless. A commercial on television triggered me and made me think everyone I loved was going to abandon me. My wife did not respond to something the way I thought she should, and I believed she didn't love me anymore.

This is crazy! No one should have to live like that. And, if you will wrestle with believing this one simple principle, you can be free from triggers, too. Here it is: No one can trigger you against your will. Let me say it again. No one can say or do anything that has the power to trigger you unless you give them that power. Yes, I said it. You control—or fail to control—being triggered by someone else's words or actions. No one can control your brain or what you think and feel.

Now, those of us that have endured trauma or that carry around unresolved pain do not believe that principle. But that doesn't make it not true. Those triggering events or moments have power over us because they connect to a set of beliefs or narratives that are already in our minds. For instance, my wife says something that expresses her pain or hurt. I am triggered to believe she doesn't love me anymore. That only happens because my internal narrative of worthlessness already carries that thought in my head. Her words only awakened awareness to it. But who will take responsibility for my triggers if not me? No one else is in my head, after all. If you work to unravel the narrative associated with each trigger you suffer, you can unravel its power over you.

Our culture fights so hard to keep up the external appearances of our facade, the image we want the world to see and believe that we are. We want to have that perfect "social media" life that is the envy of all our friends. I did it. For me, it wasn't so much the pride of wanting everyone to see this perfect life in me, it was that I genuinely desired the fullness of that life of joy, peace, love, and, at least, near perfection. I came to believe that if I could not defeat that internal monster of fear, shame, and pain, then I would build an external life that would someday overpower it. But it just does not work that way. It is still a facade covering up chaos. I would never be free until I recalled all the energy used to maintain the facade and redeployed it to face down my destructive story. It took a paradigm shift in the way I saw myself and my past experiences. It took seeing the world in front of me in a whole new way. Let us lay that foundation to begin the journey of discovering the potential our narrative holds for healing.

Strong Foundations are Only as Good as Their Footings

Before we move into section two and work on healing the damage done by past trauma and our limiting beliefs, let us be sure we understand what this foundation of freedom looks like. A good foundation is only strong if it contains solid footings. This cement-work principle is very important in our mental health as well. We need to be sure that the foundation we build to move forward in life contains these solid footings or truths. Being sure we have dismantled everything that the pain and lies of our hacked narrative built is imperative for true healing in life. We wouldn't build a house with a mix of solid wood and rotted wood; likewise, we cannot build a healed and healthy life mixed with lies and truths about who we are.

Belief: You can learn facts all day long and proclaim that you know something is good for you, but nothing will ever happen until you believe in those facts. I am convinced that knowing never elicits action, but that it takes belief to stir us to move or change. At the beginning of this book, I stated that belief was very powerful. It can build up and it can destroy. If you think about it, there is no such thing as "unbelief." There may be things we do not believe in, but that means we usually believe in something opposite or different. For years, I did not believe I deserved to be loved or to feel true joy. I wanted it. I pursued it. I even danced with it for periods of my life. But I never fully believed in it because I believed I was worthless and unlovable. I knew what God said about who I was, but even that wasn't powerful enough to set me free until I *believed* in it.

A great struggle that survivors of trauma often have is the fear of moving forward until they have 100 percent belief that everything will work out perfectly. Therefore, a lot of trauma survivors stay stuck. They desire to make a move toward freedom but, looking out at the horizon of their choices, they don't believe it will all work out the way they want. Remember, they have survival brain. Unfortunately, that means they stay where they are. Do you want to know how I finally found freedom? I stopped thinking I had to master the whole of my journey, that I had to have belief for every step. I put every ounce of my energy into believing in my next best step. And when I achieved that, I repeated the process. I pray you can begin your journey to freedom and healing by believing in your next best step.

Vulnerability: I often ask clients what they think when they hear the word *vulnerability*. The most common answer I get is weakness or danger. Our culture has taught us to hide pain; you pick yourself up by your own bootstraps. Asking for help is a weakness. This is most true among us men. A man never shows vulnerability. We must be tough. We must fix our own messes. This, of course, is all a big lie. It is so destructive. I work with so many couples whose marriages are in shambles because they fear vulnerability, and it is most often the husband. I lived this way for forty years. I feared vulnerability. The strange thing is, I helped other people embrace this for many years while I felt worthless and undeserving. I let myself believe that if I was tough enough as I helped others, I would eventually be free. Here is the truth about vulnerability. If you are on the battlefield, it can be deadly. If you are in the sports arena, it can cause you to lose the game. If you are on a jungle safari, it can be dangerous. But vulnerability in most areas of our lives is a strength, not a weakness. Vulnerability means being brave enough to embrace our story, brave enough to share it with others, and brave enough to know that it fuels the movement forward into freedom and healing.

Now: I struggled with staying in the moment for many years during my battle with my past. It was an uncomfortable place to be. It was where the monster resided, and the painful presence of my hacked narrative played on repeat. But this present moment is the only one we truly exist in. Right now. Right here. I learned to defeat my past and master the internal narrative of my future by bringing it all into the present. A lot of people think trauma recovery is laying on the proverbial couch and going back into their past. This is not true. Trauma work that brings real recovery brings everything into the present where we, and all our resources, reside. Remember this: I know your present can be an uncomfortable place if you struggle with hacked narratives and monsters in your head, but never forget that you created those. And, with the right words, you can defeat them here and now.

Buts: A lot of clients laugh at me when I tell them to get their "buts" out of here. Note the missing "t" and you'll understand the buts I mean. When I awakened to my own internal narrative, I learned that it was ravaged with buts. I could deal with such-and-such an issue, *but* I will probably fail. I would love to have more joy, *but* I am worthless and do not deserve it. I want to work on being a better husband and father, *but* I will never be enough. Many mental health struggles are fraught with this line of thinking. Most of what comes on the backside of the "but" is restrictive or damaging to our health and success. Think about your internal narrative. Be vulnerable with the truth of what you speak inside. Share with a professional or an accountability partner. Do the work to get the "buts" out of your process of pursuing freedom and healing.

Constructs: Much of what we feel powerless about are things we had a hand in creating ourselves. Fear and shame were the twin demons inside my mind. I feared the fear and shame. I never felt worthy or powerful enough to face them. That is until I learned this: fear, like triggers, was something I was more responsible for than I ever thought. Again, upon awakening an awareness of my internal narrative, I began to

WE ARE ALL FIREFLIES

easily see that I feared certain things because of the story I led myself to believe about those things. I am convinced that people do not fear spiders, yet they fear the story they tell themselves about those spiders. *He is going to kill me. He is going to sprout wings, chase me down, and poison me. They are all deadly and want to harm me.* That is a hacked narrative about spiders that can be easily defeated by learning the truth about them and by learning to respect that truth. The same is true for those hacked internal narratives and the fear and shame they nurture. My fear and shame were present and debilitating because of the things I believed about myself. When I learned to unravel those and get free from the limiting beliefs, the fear and shame died off. They never had power over me. Like triggers, they had the power I gave them, the power I allowed them to have through my beliefs.

Dismantling: Challenge every belief that has held you in bondage. If you struggle to believe fully in yourself, then believe in yourself for this moment, for your next best step. Challenge anything that brings you pain or sparks fear, shame, or anxiety. It is only a narrative, comprising hacked beliefs born out of your past trauma or painful experiences. It does not mean they are true. Feelings are also not the truth. They are just feelings.

Reject the standard of perfection. You are enough. If you struggle to see that, then connect with a professional or trusted friend who can help bring clarity. The battle is yours. There is no trauma, no pain, no fear, no poor choice, and no level of shame that cannot be redeemed. There are no experiences that cannot be used to lead us to learn, find freedom, and discover who we are meant to be. Your story is yours. It is time to stop letting it write you, and for you to begin writing your story. You deserve it, and the world needs it. The world needs your redeemed story.

You carry all the light you will ever need to illuminate all the darkness you will ever face.

Believe in that for this moment. Now, let us begin the healing.

EMBRACING LIGHT

- Embrace the power of "It is what it is." Let it help focus only on the things you can control. Let it help you embrace the moment you are in, even if it is painful. This moment is the only one you can control.

- Speak your truth. It may hurt at first, but remember, it is a healing pain. The pain and bondage in our story only have power in the darkness. Bring them to light and you begin to regain power over your story.

- Words create worlds. I may repeat that mantra one hundred times before we finish this journey. Much of what we struggle with has its power in hacked narratives inside us. Remember: if words can create painful and scary worlds, then they can be used to dismantle those worlds and create new ones full of freedom, joy, and peace.

- Perfection is a myth. Stop spending all your energy on trying to be perfect, or worse yet, staying stuck because you are waiting for perfection. Instead, use all that energy to embrace your next best step and become better than you were yesterday.

- Embrace the truth of the monsters, triggers, and facades that are holding you in bondage. You created them with your internal narrative about the painful experiences you had. Smile at the monster, take ownership of the narrative that feeds your triggers, stop polishing the facade you think the world wants to see, and just be you.

- If belief in yourself has been a battle, then work to believe in yourself for this moment and then repeat ad infinitum. Embrace vulnerability as the most courageous thing you can do to move into the life of freedom and peace you desire and deserve.

PART TWO

Reclaiming Your Present

Wonder is about having admiration for something beautiful and unfamiliar; like rediscovering our true self after it has been hidden in bondage to limiting beliefs for many years. It is about making an intimate connection with the healing we need to experience to live the life we were created for.

It is about seeing how those destructive internal narratives and limiting beliefs alter the way we go about our daily lives. For many of us, we stay stuck in that place of bondage for so long that we don't even realize how we are experiencing life through filters. The next four chapters are about identifying those filters and working to overcome the damage so we can see life—and ourselves—as they were always meant to be.

This process is humbling but necessary. This is where we learn to embrace vulnerability fully and see things as they really are. Healing old wounds and learning to embrace a new healthy narrative requires us to be honest and intentional about two things: where we currently are and how to get to where we need to be.

5

VISION

Healing the Way We See

*When your vision becomes more powerful than your memory,
your future becomes more powerful than your past.*
—Paul Dunn, B1G1

I remained in bondage to my hacked internal narrative for
so long that I forgot what it was like to be truly me. The
process of healing awakened me to the *wonder* of what it
was like to be free—truly free—from fear, shame, and limiting
beliefs. I used to think I was the only one that experienced
wonder at knowing myself, but I have seen it repeated countless times with clients who had lived under the burden of past
trauma and painful experiences. We believe lies about ourselves
for so long that we lose who we are.

Let me be clear, this was not an overnight transformation.
I did not go to sleep one night in bondage and darkness and
wake up the next day completely healed and free. It was a
process. There was, however, a single moment of clarity where
I remember stepping out of the darkness and into the light.
This moment happened as I sat on an outdoor bench overlooking the small lake in our backyard. I had just returned

from my time with an amazing counselor and new friends in Minnesota. I had a boatload of learning to unpack from my trip. There was a calm fall breeze blowing, and the leaves danced across the sky, landing on the surface of the water like an armada of small ships. It was a good day to experience complete peace, but my peace was cut with the heaviness of the work that lay before me. I had become fully aware of the monster and the hacked narrative I had carried inside me for so long. While I felt free from all of that for the first time in my life, I was also keenly aware of the damage that had been done and the work that was before me. It was like being in a completely dark room for a long time and walking straight out into the midday sun. It was bright and beautiful, but it hurt my eyes; it was hard to see. I had a vision of myself back at the crossroads that I mentioned in the introduction. I was not full of pain and hopelessness like before. This time, I knew the way. I could clearly see the path of healing that I needed to take, but I could also see the path of destruction I had left behind. It may sound crazy, but I felt like I was in the middle of nowhere and everywhere all at the same time.

I was an equal distance from the prison I had spent forty years in and the complete healing I now believed I deserved. If you have worked through trauma in your own life, I think you can identify with this place. It is where we take that last step of courage out of the old ways and the first step of faith in the newness of life. Can you relate? If you are wrestling through your own struggle with the darkness and pain of past trauma and long to step out into the light, take heart. Freedom is within your reach. You have within you the power to find your awakening and step into the wonder of who you were created to be. I believe in you.

I had to come to terms with the path of pain and damage that I could see behind me so that I could move forward into my full potential. There were moments, early in the process, when I struggled to feel worthy of this healing. The pain of my childhood abuse was with me daily, but so, too, was the pain I caused so many people by holding on to my bondage for so long. Taking my eyes off the negative and looking forward to the potential for all the positives healing would bring me was the hardest paradigm shift in this whole journey. The only way I was able to believe in my worth was to *believe for the moment.*

I think that has been the key to this whole process. Sometimes it is hard seeing the big picture. Going from the place of hopelessness I lived in for so long to believing in the whole journey of freedom and healing was near impossible. I focused my faith *in the moment.* I wrestled with my past *in the moment.* And, more than anything, I embraced the wonder of the process *in the moment.* I could not move backward any longer. I could not stay stuck in this place any longer. Forward was my only option. I allowed my healing to be the legacy that redeemed my past. If you find yourself at this place on your own journey, embrace truth because lies are what held you in bondage. Embrace your light because the darkness is what kept you imprisoned. Work hard to see with the eyes of your soul and not just your physical eyes. If you struggle with belief and faith, then have belief and faith only for the present moment. The only way *better* will come is for you to believe in it even when, *in the moment,* things aren't great.

The Fog Lifted, So Why Can't I See Clearly?

Like I said earlier, I know we would like to be able to move instantly from bondage to complete healing in one moment, but it just doesn't work that way very often. The only "light switch" experience I had was that moment of clarity in stepping out of the darkness of my past and seeing the light of possibilities for my freedom and healing in front of me. Attaining the fullness of those things was a process. Besides, as much as I would love to deny it, most of my growth came in the hard work through each step of the journey. Sure, I begged God to flip the switch for me. Who wouldn't want the easy way? But I do not see Him working that way too often. The Apostle Paul asked God to remove the thorn (struggle) from his flesh, and God responded by telling him to rely on His grace for the journey (2 Cor. 12:7–9).

The work of healing was not the same kind of battle, thankfully, as trying to move through life in bondage. Before, I was fighting against myself, fighting against that monster I had created and the internal narrative that continually beat me down. It was brutal. For many trauma survivors still in bondage, every step forward is met with one or two steps backward. That describes forty years of my life—stuck, in pain, and putting on a smile. But now, stepping into the light of awakening and potential, the healing process is not brutal; it is beautiful. Sure, it has its moments of pain. Those old narratives try to pull you back into the prison of fear and shame. I heard that voice for many months during my healing, but I continued to embrace the moment and speak the truth, and it grew fainter and fainter.

Allowing our focus to be on our pain and brokenness for so long damages our vision—the way we see the world and ourselves. When I felt the freedom from bondage, I was ready to be happy and pain-free. I was full of joy, but I was not free from pain. The good news is that healing pain is constructive, not destructive like I had experienced for so long. My past continually tore me down from the inside out. The healing process is about renewing and rebuilding. I could handle that kind of pain. Think of this part of the process as rehab, like physical therapy for the heart and mind. The first parts of my vision I worked on were my perspective, perception, and ridding myself of the blind spots I had been living with.

Our perspective is damaged from the years of negativity and, in my case at least, self-hate. Also, our perceptions become skewed by the limiting beliefs we embrace. We develop blind spots to avoid looking at things that are too painful to see.

Once I started the process of healing, I noticed I had a very poor perspective on things. I could be optimistic about anyone and anything except myself. My perspective was that the world was a great place where I could rent space but never own. In other words, I still fought to feel worthy of belonging. I continued to beat myself up by refusing to think I deserved a life like others had.

How did I combat this? Every time I had this feeling, I spoke the truth about it. I know I sound like a broken record, but the truth is what breaks the habits of believing in the lies. I asked myself, "Do you truly not deserve this, or do you only *feel* as if you don't deserve it?" I would remind myself that my experiences were just that—experiences. They did not define me. My past did not define me. I could not allow myself to stay stuck in the perspective of my darkest pain or my worst mistake. I would never see the world around me as I should from those places. Besides, God hadn't abandoned me to stay stuck there, so why should I do it to myself? In the moment, I allowed myself baby steps in having as positive a point of view toward myself as I did the world. It felt new and awkward, but I embraced it. I must have prayed a million times, *God, show me the world and myself through your eyes.* It was painful, and it was beautiful. Being vulnerable before God is the most courageous and empowering thing you can do.

Our perceptions of things are fueled by our past, our experiences, and our thoughts. When I first learned this, I thought, oh great, the things I have struggled with for most of my life are the things that affect how I perceive the world around me. *Will I ever see things clearly?* And of course, I did not see clearly at first. I battled for months against the old ways of thinking and understanding the world around me. Perceptions are where we interpret our reality. It forms our beliefs about what is true. For many years, I perceived I was worthless; I perceived I did not deserve joy and peace, and I perceived danger at every turn. This kept me stuck in false beliefs about who I was, stuck in the perpetual poor choices that relegated me to a place of worthlessness. I overcame this struggle by slowing down the process of seeing the world around me. I questioned everything—in a good way. If any perception was negative or painful, I wrote it down so I could see it with my eyes. By the way, I journaled incessantly during my whole journey. I highly recommend it. Writing down my perceptions allowed me to differentiate real from imagined and true in the past from true now. It was an arduous process. You must stay the course if you are to ever find a healthy perception of yourself and the world.

During my bondage, blind spots served me well—or so I thought. Trauma survivors develop blind spots to avoid anything that can cause more pain or send us into a spiral of the fear and shame narrative. I was a master at developing and nurturing them. I used blind spots to avoid anyone knowing I was in pain or struggling with anxiety. I felt too unworthy of anyone knowing. Sadly, I think I was pretty good at hiding it. I built walls around things that brought me fear. Being afraid of almost everything, you can imagine how crowded my life was with walls and blind spots. I also turned away from anything that I could not understand, that reminded me of my past, or especially (since I am a man), anything I could not fix.

Those blind spots made a troubled part of my story more palpable at one time, but to allow them to linger caused me to miss things that could speed my healing and growth. I had more courage at this stage in my journey, so what did I do with my blind spots? I attacked them. I ran straight into them. After all, I now knew that I wrote the narratives that supported these things. I did not need to be afraid. I was not still being abused. I was not worthless. If I felt something painful or scary, I embraced it as a feeling, not my reality. I slowly but surely dismantled the filters. And, in doing so, I learned that the things I feared most and avoided the hardest were what brought the most healing.

Will the Authentic Reality Please Stand Up?

Unprocessed trauma can be debilitating in many ways, but one way that causes much confusion and pain is how it alters our view of reality. This is one of the core struggles for those experiencing post-traumatic stress disorder (PTSD). I was working with a sexual abuse/addiction counselor in Dallas during part of my healing journey, and I remember the day he told me, "I think you have dealt with PTSD most of your life." It was the first time I had heard that, and I did not like it. I was so uncomfortable with that diagnosis that I am just now mentioning it in my book. I guess I feared labels because I had put so many negative ones on myself most of my life. I had worked with clients with PTSD, most of whom were military veterans. I am a peacetime military veteran and for some reason, I did not feel worthy to include myself in a struggle our brave soldiers coped with. I know that was short-sighted on my part. As a matter of fact, I had known other clients with PTSD who never served in the military. I guess it was just the residual effect of me feeling worthless—I wasn't important enough to have a "real" problem. His diagnosis helped me greatly in my healing. It helped me to see how my view of reality had gotten so skewed. More correctly, it helped me to see I was living in three separate realities. No wonder my internal self-talk was so crazy at times.

Of course, I was living in *the* reality, but at the same time, I was existing in a *desired* reality and a *believed* reality. When you live in a state of chaos born out of unresolved trauma, it is common to create other ideals for your life that are less painful than the one you are living. My reality was painful. It represented a world that I felt I could never live up to, a world where I felt like a fraud in my being worthless and unlovable. I fought to fit in, and in many ways, I did. I kept the facade of happiness and peace polished and shiny. But I was constantly broken under the weight of it all.

My desired reality was my dream world. It was the one where I saw only the good. I called it my world of unicorns, fireflies, and smiles. Sounds a bit childish for an adult, doesn't it? That's because it was the creation of a mind frozen at a childish stage by early trauma. My desired world was where I retreated when the monster attacked, and my internal narrative exploded in a cacophony of shame and hate for myself. Looking back, I can see where this saved me from going deeper down the rabbit hole, but I can also see where it helped keep me in bondage. It allowed me to avoid facing my actual reality.

My believed reality was my hell. It was the one that encompassed the real pain I endured from sexual abuse and my lifelong struggle with poor choices. It also included the lies, the self-hate, and the full belief that being worthless and unlovable was my truth, my cross to bear. In short, it is where the monsters lived, and it was where I lived most of my life.

How did I correct this? One way was born naturally through the process of awakening to my internal narrative. As I began to see how much of my fear, shame, and the pain was due to my own self-imposed beliefs, my desired and believed realities were exposed as the fantasy worlds they were. The other way I healed this part of my vision was more intentional. I learned to question everything. This process was awkward at first, but our minds function very efficiently and very fast, so I worked hard to develop it into a habit that became second nature.

If I doubted the way I was seeing or perceiving things around me, I followed this line of questioning:

- *Is it true?* Shining truth into the darkness is simple, yet profound in its effectiveness. This is not *thinking* something is true, nor is it *wanting* something to be true. It's about *being* true. It is good to have a trusted professional or friend to help with this part.

- *Is it happening now?* This question is imperative for trauma survivors and anxiety sufferers. We get easily lost in our thoughts and feelings. It may remind us of something that happened in the past or make us experience the feelings when something bad happened, but if it isn't happening now, we need not respond to it.

- *Is there value in accepting or wrestling with this view?* How do you know? My rule of measure is this: can it teach me, and does it move me forward? In other words, does it help me in my journey of becoming a better version of my yesterday self? If not, let it go.

I hope that gives you some help in keeping yourself grounded. We do not have to fight or wrestle with every thought or feeling that comes along and skews our perceptions or perspective. Embracing the reality of our story is hard, but it is the only true path to the freedom and healing we deserve.

The Three Sees

One last thing I worked to recognize and raise awareness of is what I call the three sees. They are

- how I see the world around me,

- how I see myself within the world, and

- how I perceive the world sees me.

All three of these views are usually battered and beaten in trauma survivors, especially when they deal with intense anxiety. When I first started the process of healing, I scored a failing grade in all three of these areas. What is the good news? I knew what had caused it. I just had to unravel years of negative thinking.

How I see the world. My issue with how I saw the world, as I said before, was never about how I felt about others. It was never negative. My view of the world was that it represented something unattainable for me, something I could only occasionally enjoy a taste of before it was taken from me. To overcome this, I had to be very intentional about listening well to others and my own voice. I only focused on things that helped me embrace my now—my true, real, and authentic now. What we search for the hardest is what we most often find. I always saw the negative in things. Without even knowing it, I searched for things that supported my broken view of self and my worthlessness. I thought if I gave into the chaos and lies, there would be some balance. *Just believe the lies, and you don't have to fight it anymore.* I am so glad to be free from that. I challenged myself to consume all positive things. When I saw or felt something negative, I combatted it by looking at or thinking about two positive things. I journaled positive observations daily by the dozens. I spoke positive observations to anyone that would listen. Let me be clear: I was not candy-coating my false beliefs with alternative, wishful falsehoods about how the world was. I was combatting many years of my brain being on autopilot in seeing the negative by forcing it to think true, positive thoughts. We *can* rewire and retrain our brains. I surrounded myself with a few key people that constantly reminded me of the truth—the truth of who I was and what I deserved. You know the saying: it takes a village.

How I see myself in the world. This one is easy: I didn't. I acted like I fit in. I showed up. I have always had tons of friends, been involved in lots of social and community activities, and worked hard to connect to others. But I experienced it all from the belief that it was only my desired world, and I had to take what I could get. It is simple. People who struggle with feeling worthless will live as if they are worthless until that thought is challenged and changed. I chose to not allow any negativity during my healing process. To this day, I work hard to protect my mind and heart from the negative things in the world. I am not saying I changed this by seeing the world through rose-colored glasses and pretending there was no negative. I just chose to not allow it into my thoughts or perceptions. I made sure I saw myself in the present moment and did not allow any dwelling on the past. I had to. If I kept beating myself up for being abused or making bad choices, I would stay stuck forever. It was all about showing myself the grace I so easily showed everyone around me. I reminded myself that feelings are just feelings. I used the three-step line of questioning I mentioned above and pressed into seeing only truth, not perceived truth, or desired truth, but actual truth. And then I hung my hat on that. This was also a step in which I included my circle of family and friends to help me.

How the world sees me. Wow, this one is a struggle for more than just trauma survivors and anxiety sufferers. Much of the world is obsessed with what people think about them. Social media has helped to stir this into a frenzy of epidemic proportions. I want to be blunt here and say it like this: "Who gives a rat's ass what other people think? Be yourself." Sure, I use what some would say is a little more colorful language here to get the point across. But it is true, especially for those of us trying to heal our internal narrative and to break free from the bondage of worthlessness, not being enough, or feeling like a failure. If you worry about what others think, you will never find complete freedom and healing. Have one or a few trustworthy advocates and/or a professional in your circle of healing and release yourself from the pressure to measure up to everyone else.

Oh, and that goes double for your social media world. Almost everyone there is polishing their facades. You will always find people that think you are too broken, too healed, too happy, too sad, etc. But to those that matter, you are loved, and you are perfect, even with your imperfections. You are enough. Embrace yourself and give yourself a measure of grace for the moment. Work to become a better version of yourself than you were yesterday.

Embracing Light

- Embrace the wonder in your journey of healing. Be amazed by the new and mysterious things you can learn in the moment.

- Stop living as if your past is still happening to you. Yes, healing can be painful and scary, but remember, some of your greatest growth comes from those things you feared and avoided.

- Is it true? Is it happening now? Is there value in accepting or wrestling with this? Make sure what you allow in does two things: teaches you something and moves you forward.

- Allow your healing to be the legacy that redeems your past.

- The only way *better* will come is to believe in it even when, in that moment, things are not great.

- Be aware of your vision. You will always find those things you seek for the hardest. Be sure they are things that help you become a better version of yourself.

6

VOICE

Healing the Way We Hear

We suffer more in imagination than in reality.
—Seneca

I shared earlier that, for much of my life, I hated my internal voice. I couldn't trust it. It kept me in bondage to fear and shame. It kept me in chaos. For years, I tried to shut it down as best I could. The problem that arose, as a result, is that I forgot how to communicate with myself. I forgot how to listen to my inner voice.

My freshman-year psychology professor once asked whether anyone in the class believed in hypnosis. All the class, except me and one girl, raised their hands. He then looked at us and said, "If you two let me hypnotize you as a part of my doctoral studies, I will give you one hundred on your test scores." He wanted nonbelievers for his study. *Where do I sign up?*

I didn't know what to expect as he began the process of hypnotizing me. To my later surprise, he succeeded in putting me under. The experience was a blur. I had crazy visions of family. Some images of my abuse came to mind. But the thing that stuck out most was a large figure standing on a hill saying, "Don't worry, Travis. I am here with you." I left his office thinking it was a neat trick but not giving it much more thought.

Two years later, I fell out of the upper story of the fraternity house after a night of binge drinking. During the time the paramedics were attending to me, the large figure reappeared. This time, he was surrounded by light and said the same thing, "Don't worry, Travis. I am here with you."

A couple of decades after that, I was in Tennessee, sitting on a large boulder on the side of a mountain. I was having a yelling match with myself and God, agonizing over where the abuse and my poor choices had led me. And there it was again, among the trees. This time, it was just a voice. "Don't worry, Travis. I am here with you." Silence. I knew the voice. It wasn't like a friend or family member, but it was just so familiar. This time, the words sunk deep into me, and I *heard* them; I embraced them. It was God speaking to my soul. I know some of you reading this book may not believe in God or believe that He speaks to us. I respect that. I just know what I know about my experiences and have faith that he was offering me the guidance I needed all along. It just took forty years for me to hear Him.

And I needed to hear Him because He was assuring me, I would survive facing down the darkness inside me. Whether it is hearing from God or listening well to our own voice, we must engage with ourselves. We must make it a habit to practice good listening and healthy connecting to our inner voices. You cannot master an internal narrative that you do not fully understand.

Don't Go There

Listening to our internal narrative sometimes means knowing what things *not* to listen to. I said hundreds of things to myself throughout the years that helped keep me stuck and beholden to limiting beliefs. But I want to mention three themes that recurred for me, and I have witnessed them to be a struggle for many of my traumatized clients. These habitual narratives all work to keep us focused on the negatives or the things we cannot control, and they lead us to ineffective ways to manage our trauma recovery.

Why me? There were times I was so tired of fighting the incessant battle with fear and shame that I felt like everything out of my mouth was a complaint. I must have said, "Why me?" a million times. If we are not careful, the negativity wrought out of constant complaining can spill over into every area of our lives. For me, it did two things. The complaining did indeed permeate every area of my life. But there were certain parts of my life that were very special to me, and I fought the complaining with what I call obsessive positivity. Does that make sense? I would insist, in these areas, that everything work out positively, that everyone involved was happy, successful, and at peace. If they weren't, then I blamed myself. The monster inside reminded me. *Why are you trying to do that? You know you are worthless. You know you will fail.* I let him be right more times than I like to admit.

Overcompensating for a complaining and negative spirit rarely works for very long. Here is what I finally decided about complaining: it is like using a fishnet to try to fill a bucket with water. There is a lot of effort put forth, a lot of energy wasted, and you look kind of silly doing it. You will never fill the bucket using a fishnet, and you will never move forward in life by complaining.

Do you struggle with a complaining or a negative spirit? Here's a tip: do not be too hard on yourself. Beating yourself up for it will just keep you in a loop of shame and self-hate. Own the narrative, raise your awareness to areas where complaining is a habit, and then work to replace it with positive and affirming words.

I feel, so I am. If I feel it, then it must be true, right? I say that sarcastically, but I struggled with this for many years. If I let someone down, I would not only feel the pain of failure, but I would also conclude that I *was* a failure. Or I would feel as if I had not pleased someone or made them happy, and I took it as more evidence that I had no worth. Those feelings of worthlessness were always right below the surface, tucked safely away behind my smile.

I remember a shift taking place early in my marriage. I do not know exactly what started the shift, but I think it was the pressure I put on myself for having this family who loved me and looked up to me now. I never told my mom and dad about the abuse because I held on to the childhood belief that everyone would leave me if I told them, and they would discover I was worthless. Now, I had this amazing wife who loved me. I gave her my heart but kept my dark past a secret for most of our marriage. I no longer struggled with merely feeling worthless, I now constantly said to myself, *I am worthless*. It was my identity. Once that thought planted in my mind, it became my go-to statement to explain anything painful. If I feel it, then it must be true.

If you know this phenomenon, please hear me: it is *not* true. It is tragically far from the truth. Feelings are just feelings. That's it, pure and simple. They eventually go away or change, which means they only represent a temporary state. Feelings cannot define your identity unless you allow them.

If___, then___. I remember enjoying using if-then statements in math and computer science classes in college. If *this* happens, then *that* will happen. They are not inherently bad in any way. If you are hungry, then eat something. If you are tired, then sleep. But in the mind of someone who struggles with hacked narratives from trauma, anxiety, or other painful experiences, they can become a destructive force. If-then statements are usually at work in our subconscious narrative. For trauma survivors, such statements often support addictions and unhealthy habits. That is where I first noticed them in the work to understand my own internal narrative. I never remember them being a conscious thought; I just saw the effects. If you feel anxious, then drink and quiet the voices. If you feel worthless, then go try to save the world. I could list hundreds. Hindsight really is 20/20.

How then can you avoid forty years of suffering and identify this process that happens subconsciously? It takes working backward through your if-then condition. You deal with the *then* first. Say you struggle with excessive drinking; you know it has become destructive for you, and you want to stop. You must work to awaken the narrative just before the event. What caused you to feel as if you needed to drink? You may say to yourself, *I was trying to please my boss, but I constantly felt like a failure.* Maybe another time you drank too much; you recall trying to plan a trip for your family, and you felt like a failure because you forgot a huge detail. You could work to awaken an awareness of more similar experiences. But in this example, it seems clear that the if-then at work goes something like this: *If I feel like a failure, then I drown my thoughts in alcohol.* Knowing this connection, we can stop the futile fight with the *then*—in this case, excessive drinking—and put our effort into eliminating the *if* in the equation, feeling like a failure.

These are just three common examples of how hacked narratives can become destructive in our daily lives. A lot of our pain and dysfunction is supported and/or exacerbated by the lies and limiting beliefs harbored in our story. Therefore, awakening to our own narrative is vitally important to our healing. And remember, you have your conscious voice and your unconscious voice at work in your mind. To know yourself is to free yourself. Spend time each day just sitting with your inner narrative. Do not be judgmental. Do not allow yourself to hate or try to solve everything. Just listen. Speak out loud to yourself. Ask questions. Your unconscious voice will only awaken if you are intentional about connecting to it. And I will probably say it ten more times, but journaling what that inner voice is saying is also very powerful. Surround yourself with a small group of trusted friends who you can be vulnerable with, and if you struggle with unprocessed pain or trauma, add a coach or counselor to your circle. Make sure they are experienced in trauma recovery.

Trauma Demands to Be Heard—Until…

I was working with a couple several years ago who came to get help with the husband's anger problem. Things almost got out of control several times, and they were afraid it was going to end their marriage. I challenged them to discuss the most recent anger outburst.

He shared, "I had come home from a hard day of work, kicked off my shoes at the front door, and walked down the hallway to my bedroom. Halfway down the hall, I stepped on one of my boy's Lego™ pieces. I lost it. Do you know how bad those things hurt on bare feet? I yelled at them to come and pick up their toys. I told them I was tired of repeating myself about keeping their things put where they belong."

His wife saw it differently. "You were screaming, cussing, and spitting in their faces. They were afraid. You yelled at me. You were out of control."

Judging by his posture, I could tell he knew she was right. I agreed with him that Legos are very painful on bare feet, but I asked if he thought his anger response was appropriate for the situation.

"Hell, no," he said, "My kids are going to hate me if I don't stop being so angry. What is wrong with me?"

"What were you feeling just before the anger outburst? What were you really that angry about?" I asked.

He told me he felt they were being disrespectful by not picking up their toys after being told. As he talked about how the workday had gone, he said his boss had upset him and made him feel disrespected by giving a big project to another employee with less time on the job.

"So, you get angry anytime you feel disrespected?"

"Yes.".

"What do you fear most in life?" I asked. He joked about being fearless and tried to change the subject. He continued with general banter for about fifteen minutes and then got a serious look on his face. I could tell he knew the answer to the question.

With tears forming in his eyes he said, "I hate my anger, but I hate being disrespected even more. It makes me feel like I am not enough for anyone. I feel like I have never been enough and never will be."

There it was. He had uncovered his trauma narrative. It is most often hidden behind our core fears. It took more than one visit to get to the precipice event where this narrative was born, but we got there. He shared how he knew his parents loved him growing up, but his dad had never told him how proud he was of him. He said he never remembered anything but negative from his father. He could never measure up. His grades were not good enough, and he wasn't a starter on the football team like his dad was. But the day came that he was going to start in a game. He told his dad about it, but he said he could not get free from work. When he walked into the house after the game, his dad was in his recliner watching television. He had not worked late as he said was required. Before he could share his excitement for how he had played, his dad said, "Well, how many times did you fumble the ball?" That was it. He decided he would never please his father. He would never be enough for anyone.

Here are two core truths about trauma:

1. Seemingly small events can poison our narrative for many years. Remember, trauma is less about the

experience and more about the story we write and believe about that experience.

2. Trauma will stay with you until you do the work to resolve it. Emotional responses, like the core event experience, will awaken the old trauma and the years of limiting beliefs we have held about it.

We all feel pain in acknowledging bondage, especially from things that happened many years ago. We feel like failures and as if we are broken. This is especially true for us men. We dislike admitting we had experiences that stirred emotions in us, or we could not fix. Therefore, far fewer men get help with trauma, especially sexual abuse trauma. I pray my story can help at least one man find freedom.

The husband in this story hated that such a "small event" (his words) had derailed his life. But he pressed into his story and did the hard work. We met together for six months. Like I said earlier, the experience for him was brutal, but it was beautiful. He defeated his monsters, he uncovered his limiting beliefs, and he found freedom and healing. Here's the deal: trauma demands to be heard. It will awaken when similar emotional experiences remind our brain of the trauma event. That is why a little anger becomes a lot, and a little anxiety becomes overwhelming. Our stories long for resolution. Trauma demands to be heard, to be faced. It might be painful, but it will be freeing. Let me remind you of the core truth of this book: you carry all the light you will ever need to illuminate all the darkness you will ever face.

If You Don't Like Where You Are, Then Listen

Our core beliefs tell us who we are and how to feel about it. For much of my life, I told myself I was worthless, so I believed it and I acted like it. When I worked through my journey of freedom and healing, I found worth and belief in myself. Guess what? I started to act like I was worthy, and I started to believe I deserved it. Negative cognitions and affirmations have one huge thing in common; they are both very powerful. Remember the mantra I shared at the beginning of the book: words create worlds. It is so true. I love to see those I am blessed to work with awakening to this truth. As in my own journey, I tell them if you do not like where you are in life, stop and listen to your internal narrative. Our core beliefs are like a seed factory, and life is the fertile soil where things grow. That was very humbling to me when I first learned it. I was sexually abused. I struggled with addictions and poor choices because of it. But the heaviest thing to process was recognizing that much of my pain was created and nurtured by my own internal narrative, my seed factory.

Our brains have a filter that helps to manage this seed factory. It is the reticular activating system (RAS). It helps us to focus on things.[5] Very few of our thoughts and narratives are held in our consciousness. Like an iceberg, much of what the brain is doing for us is below the surface. That is also where much of our internal narrative is held, the good and the bad. I do not want to go all science class on you here, but this is how I came to understand its inner workings. Remember how great hindsight is? Looking back through my narrative, I noticed that every time I felt bad, struggled with anxiety, or made poor life choices, there was a self-created narrative at work. The brain holds our focus on what we tell it is important.

Here is a very simple, relatable illustration. I had a red Ford F-150™ for almost fifteen years. I loved that truck, but it was starting to give me problems, and it made me think. *I am not getting any younger, so maybe it is time to get my bucket list vehicle.* I searched around and found it: a Hydro Blue Pearl 2015 Jeep Wrangler™ soft top. My wife and I love dropping the top and taking rides out in the countryside. Guess what my brain's RAS filter did? It said, *hey, he loves Jeeps now, especially blue ones. Let's point out every one of them he crosses paths with.* Maybe for you, it was a coat, a pair of shoes, or even a phone case. You notice things more when they become important to you. The filter listens to our narrative, identifies the main themes, and loads them up into our consciousness and focus. So, if you struggle with unresolved trauma and pain and think about it daily, guess what the brain will do? Yep, it will remind us of the things we are telling it we want to focus on, even our pain.

Now we see why it is so hard to get free from that bondage and those negative core self-beliefs. We grow best what we nurture the most. If I have a garden and nurture the tomato plants more than the weeds, I will get tomatoes. The converse is also true. And in our thought life, if we nurture negative thoughts more than positive thoughts, that is what we will get. If you struggle with unresolved trauma, please know that you have far more control over your inner voice than you can imagine. It takes time to break old "thinking" habits. You must show yourself some grace and have faith in the process. Remember, your internal dialogue will determine your external direction. Don't like where you are headed? Work at the root, the narrative, and you can change that direction. Again, journal through the process and work with a professional trained in trauma recovery.

The Thought-Feeling-Emotion Dynamic

Before we finish this chapter, I want to talk just a little about the very basic parts of our internal voice: our thoughts, feelings, and emotions. I could write a whole book on the topic of this section alone. Maybe, one day I will.

Our thoughts, feelings, and emotions are parts of who we are. I look at it this way: they are God-given capacities that are there to help us process and make sense of the world around us. When we use them to assess situations and make sound judgments about how to feel and what to do, we are good. It's when we use them as they were not intended that we begin to have problems. Trauma survivors often do a good job of this. I was the king of misusing them for a long time.

Thoughts are simply our mental cognitions, that internal narrative or the things we put into words. They contain and influence our perceptions and perspective on ourselves and the outside world. Our emotions are the subconscious, physiological (bodily) phenomena we experience in reaction to stimuli. Feelings are the conscious awareness of emotions as filtered through our thoughts. Feelings exist in our mind.[6] Simple, right? But how are they related? Does one come before the others? Does it even matter?

There are many theories on the relationships among these, but my favorite suggests they are all interrelated and can influence one another. Thoughts can stir feelings which spark an emotional response. An external stimulus can create emotions that remind us of thoughts and feelings. Taken as a whole, this process tells us something. Good or bad, our thoughts, feelings, and emotions are informing us.[7] Whether this helps or hurts us depends on what we do with them.

The primary thing to remember is that the more cognitive or aware we are of the process of thoughts, feelings, and emotions working together, the better off we are. During my bondage, I was usually reactive to this process at best. I was like a rudderless ship in a tumultuous storm on the open sea. Thoughts and feelings would pop up and lead me wherever they wanted to take me, and I would respond and try to put the pieces back together. This was often after running aground and wrecking the ship (i.e., beating myself up and/or making poor choices).

I was able to change this years-long journey by realizing the rudder was in my hand the whole time. This wasn't an easy realization. Learning that I was in control, even of my painful and destructive narratives, led me to find the power to change directions. Does it make you feel better knowing you have conscious control over your thoughts and this whole process? Let me say this, some people do have biological conditions inside the brain that mitigate their degree of control of parts or all of this, but, for most of us, it is in our hands.

I want to just bullet-point some things I learned about thoughts, feelings, and emotions to close this chapter.

- Feelings are not facts or truth; they are just feelings.

- I do not have to respond to every feeling I have. I can just let them go.

- Feeling your feelings will rarely kill you. Avoiding them, however, almost killed me.

- Sitting with your thoughts and feelings can lead to freedom and healing. They are not there to harm you. They are usually pointing out something that needs your attention, your help—like the sore knee we talked about in chapter three.

- Showing emotion is not weakness. Do you hear that, men? Sometimes, emoting or crying can be the most cathartic and healing thing we can do.

- While thoughts are influenced by our experiences, surroundings, and environment, our internal narrative is still mostly within our conscious control. We just need to harness the power and nurture the habit of being proactive with them.

Embracing Light

- Embrace your inside voice, pain, and all. It is your ticket to freedom and healing.

- Remember: Complaining is like trying to dip a bucket of water with a fishnet. You will look silly, put in a lot of effort, and have little to show for it.

- Feelings are not facts. They are not truth. They are feelings. Listen to them, learn from them, or choose to let them go, but never take them as the gospel truth about who you are.

- Trauma demands to be heard and will continue to be a prominent part of your narrative until you face it down. Your story longs for resolution. You are more powerful than you can imagine. Face it down, learn from it, and let it go.

- If you do not like where you are in life, stop and listen. Your internal dialogue determines your external direction.

- Be intentional with your thought life. Be present with it. Journal, talk to a friend, seek out a professional. Whatever you do, be in control of it. Remember, we write our stories, or they write us.

7

VELOCITY

Healing the Way We Move

We're not all of the decisions we've made in the past;
we're what we do next, with what God's given us to work with.
—Bob Goff

There were once three frogs living on a beautiful lake. It was full of majestic cypress trees, lily pads, and the most amazing view of the sunset; well, if you lived on the other shore. One evening, the three frogs sat together, lamenting over how they longed to get a better view of the setting sun. They all decided that life would be better if they lived on the other side of the lake, so they all promised they would develop a plan to make that happen.

The first frog could not contain his excitement. He was tired of living the life he had, and he decided he deserved to live in the land of the beautiful sunsets right now. He ran around frantically on his lily pad, packed his frog suitcase, turned toward the other shore, and took one giant leap. Of course, he fell way short—oh, and into the mouth of an alligator.

The second frog was just as excited to live in the land with the beautiful views. He, too, ran around his lily pad, packing his bags. He awoke the next morning and took off hopping from one lily pad to the other, never to be seen again. Unfortunately, no one stopped him and told him the sun sets in the west, and he was last seen hopping *south*.

The third frog also looked forward to living on the other side of the lake. He thought, *life will be great, and I can enjoy the amazing sunset every night from my new lily pad*. He wanted to leave instantly as the other two frogs did, but he knew there was much planning to do for such a journey. The third frog vowed to find peace and balance on the lily pad he was currently living on and to spend his free time mapping out the best and safest journey he could. He thought, *one lily pad at a time, and I will reach my goal*.

The moral of the story is, take your time and do not get in too much of a hurry. Be patient and learn before you leap. There is much to be said for starting a great journey from a place of peace and balance. I should know; I spent many years living life like the first frog, thinking every move I made had to be quick, perfect, and a direct route to my goal. I spent quite a few years as the second frog, randomly hopping from one place in life to another, never satisfied and never at peace because I never made it to the place I sought. This is where I made most of my mistakes in life. Thankfully, I learned how to become the third frog. Embracing my story and my moments from a place of peace and balance helped me to gain the footing, courage, and strength to make it to the other side of my lake. And the sunsets are so very beautiful.

Slow Down Before You Break Something

So why use the word *velocity* for this chapter's title? Well, one reason is that I am an old physics nerd who loved studying vector analysis in college, and I also wanted all the words in part two to begin with the letter V. But there's a better reason. Velocity deals with not only speed, but also direction. When

I awakened to my hacked internal narrative, I found myself moving through life a hundred miles an hour in every direction, most of which was the wrong way. I had a velocity problem, and it was tearing me apart from the inside out. My healing had to include learning how to move through life again.

One of the greatest struggles I dealt with while under the bondage of my trauma narrative and anxiety was that I could not be still. It was hard for me to stay put in one place for very long, not just physically, but mentally and emotionally as well. I was all over the place. My parents used to just think that it was my attention deficit hyperactivity disorder (ADHD), which I have had all my life. But I learned to manage that well. The reason I tell all my clients, and anyone else who will listen, to embrace their moments is that I failed to do it for so long. I know I missed out on opportunities. I missed out on the richness of some friendships. The only place I could experience life was in the present moment, so why did I struggle with it for so long? Why did I move through life as if I were a pollen-starved bee in a world full of flowers?

Because I learned that running and never staying put in one place very long kept the monsters at bay. If I was always moving, always experiencing something new, then my mind could not hear the hacked narrative of hate, fear, and shame in my head. The only problem was that no one can keep moving 24/7. And you cannot be successful if you do not stay with something. Yet, when I slowed down or stopped moving, the voices got louder, as if they were in a rage at me for trying to leave them behind. Mind you, I knew that internal voice was me. I hadn't forgotten that I created it, and I believed in it.

I thought running from my trauma was buying me the time and space to be happy, or at least not to be tormented by my internal narrative. But what did it get me? It's not a pretty list:

- It supported the belief that I was worthless and unlovable.

- It pushed me to believe that if I stayed in one place for too long, everyone else would find out I was worthless.

- It brought the loss of a lot of opportunities because I quit jobs too often and gave up on opportunities too fast.

- It supported my lying, internal belief that if I just helped more people, led more mission trips, and started more relief projects, then joy would defeat the pain someday.

- It created a huge blind spot. I believed I was running from my pain, the monsters, and the brokenness of the trauma when I was just carrying them with me everywhere I went.

I never left jobs because I hated them. I never started new projects because the old ones stopped bringing joy. It was never because any of those things failed to be enough. It was because *I* was not enough and, for a long time, I didn't know what else to do with that pain except run.

Watch Your Language

Words create worlds. Yes, I am reminding you of it again. Why? Because it is one of the most integral and paradigm-shifting things I learned on my journey to break free from my hacked trauma narrative. We have already talked about words that create and support worlds of pain, lies, and shame. Now, let's talk about some words we need to address to heal the way we move through life. I see these come up often when working with struggling couples, but they are present in almost every client I do trauma recovery work with. It is quite common for trauma survivors to be uncomfortable with themselves; being present with yourself in the moment stirs up anxiety and pain. We do not like being alone with our monsters or with that hamster on the narrative wheel, spinning out of control in our minds. I thought I would never break the habit of moving so fast through life, thinking I had to experience everything within my grasp. The breakthrough came during the first step of my quest for freedom, when I raised my awareness of being able to hear my internal narrative. There were six words that constantly rose to the surface of the conversation, not only in my head but with others as well. We will call two of them, *always* and *never*, our terminal language. The other four of them, *would've*, *could've*, *should've*, and *what-if*, we will call our time-travel language.

I have a phrase I share with clients often: *always* and *never* are never always true. That might sound a little hokey, but it is basically the truth. I first started seeing these words pop up when working with couples in crisis. I repeatedly heard things like, "You always blame me," "You never open up to me," etc. Now, I am not saying there was not truth in such claims, but they are simply not 100 percent true or true all the time. I questioned a husband about it once.

"Does she really *always* blame you, like every time?"

"Well, not *always*, but eighty percent of the time."

"Okay, we can work with that number much better."

The words always and *never* were my go-to responses when my feelings of worthlessness were spinning out of control. "I will never please anyone. I will always be worthless," I often said these things to my wife. She gently responded with the list of accomplishments I had achieved and the number of people I had helped, and she reminded me of my worth to her and the family. Those terminal words take us to the end of the spectrum of possibilities. If I believed my always and never narratives were true, I didn't have to wrestle with hope, with being let down, and with feeling more worthless because things did not work out the way I wanted. They allowed me to continue wallowing in the prison I had created.

Always and *never* are never always true. As I began to taste freedom, I waged war against these words. I called them out every time I caught them coming out of my mouth. I journaled my thoughts. I called them into question. *Is that true?* I asked myself. If the answer was *no*, I pressed into my narrative until truth arose. I did not let myself chase an all-or-nothing perfection in this. I just learned to embrace the moment and my truth as I pursued being a better version of myself.

Do you believe in time travel? I bet some of you have done it without even knowing it. No, I do not mean physically, but mentally and emotionally. As I started working with more and more trauma and anxiety clients, I noticed those time-travel words were rampant in their narratives. *Would've, could've,* and *should've* take our minds back to the past, while *what-if* pushes us forward into the future. Do you see how that is like time traveling in our minds? One of the things that kept me from finding healing much sooner than I did was my incessant time travel into my past. *I should've avoided that; if I would've listened to my parents…; I could've had a normal childhood if those men hadn't abused me.* The power of good trauma recovery work is to bring the past into the present and challenge the hacked narratives to learn from them. That way, we are not reliving the past and drowning in the anxiety that we cannot change it, but we are processing the past in the now, so that we can change ourselves. Allowing our narrative to push us back into the past, where we cannot change anything, wastes precious mental and emotional energy, and keeps us stuck in our narratives of hopelessness. I had a professor in grad school who gave this sage advice about time-travel words: "You know how to break the habit of getting caught up in being enslaved by those words? Just stop *should-ing* all over yourself." Well, we were waiting for something a little more serious, but that works too.

There was a joke in my family that if we had a quarter for every time Travis asked *what-if* questions, we would all retire rich. I was obsessed with always asking this about every subject. When my incessant need to ask *what-if* about everything invaded the peace of a good day of fishing, my dad responded with the same answer every time. I am sure this was his ploy to shut me up.

"Dad, what if our boat floats too close to those woods where alligators live?" My Dad responded, "What if a frog had wings? He wouldn't bump his butt on the ground every time he hopped." His ploy worked. That answer confused me and shut me up—well, for the moment.

I was about twenty years old and home from college to spend a weekend with the family, and Dad and I went fishing (yes, we did a lot of fishing together). I was still obsessed with the what-ifs of my future, and when I raised one of my what-if questions, I got the same silly answer. This time I responded. "Dad, what do you mean by that silly statement?" Looking back at me like some country boy armchair philosopher, he said, "What do you think I mean?"

"I have no idea. It doesn't make any sense,"

"Exactly", he proclaimed. At that moment, I got it.

Years later, I was reminded of that moment as I sat on the bed next to my dad while he was slowly leaving his earthly body. As tears streamed down my face, I was trying to replace the piercing pain with good memories of the rich life we shared together for forty-one years. It didn't make sense to what-if my life away, worrying about a future that had not happened. Every time I did that with my anxiety and trauma pain, I created another potential future reality to have to worry about. I was nurturing fear and hopelessness for multiple realities, none of which had happened yet, and ninety-nine percent of them never would. Life is not lived in the future. Life is lived in the right now. Like my dad said the day he got the cancer diagnosis, "It is what it is." He taught me to dance in my moments, and even after losing him, that legacy helped me embrace my story and find healing.

You cannot get free from trauma by fighting a past that you cannot change or agonizing over a future that has not happened. You are not God or Captain Kirk; you cannot time travel in either direction. You certainly can't change things that have already happened or haven't happened yet. Trying to do so will only bring depression, regret, anger, and anxiety. I know, I battled them all. Embrace your story—the good, the bad, and the ugly—in the now, and work to use it to your advantage to learn and grow toward freedom and healing.

We should know one more thing about watching our language. Many who battle past trauma and anxiety struggle with trying to control everything around them, present company included. We think the more we can control, the better we will feel. The opposite is almost always true. Here is the measure of whether you are outreaching the actual control you have over things around you. You, I, and every other human on the planet control only two things:

1. The choices we make.

2. How we respond to everyone else's choices.

Everything else is either outside our control, or at best, something we can influence.

Something in the Way You Move

Be mindful of how you move through life. Be intentional with your steps. If you are battling through the bondage of past trauma or any other issue keeping you from being your best self, then you will more than likely experience one or more velocity problems. You will look up one day and be bouncing around, like I was, a hundred miles an hour in every direction, most of which will probably be wrong or destructive, as they were for me. Here are three simple best practices to develop into habits to help speed your healing in how you move through life:

- **Be still**. We live in a culture that is moving around like they are on one of those automatic sidewalks at the airport. Busyness has come to be equated with success. We must keep up with the neighbors, or at least our social media friends. The best thing you can do for your mental and physical health is to practice just sitting quietly with yourself fifteen minutes a day (not with your phone or anything else, just with yourself). I like to recite these words from Scripture (Psalm 46:10) taking a few deep breaths between each phrase, as a guide for bringing me into stillness:

  > Be still and know that I am God. (breathe)
  > Be still and know. (breathe)
  > Be still. (breathe)
  > Be. (Practice just being.)

- **Be here**. You have heard me talk about embracing your moments over and over, but it can be hard in a world that demands our focus and attention at every turn. So, I have learned to practice being present intentionally. Pick something to focus on—a sunset, a puppy playing in the yard, your children, a flower, or anything really. Notice it; do not just look at it. Use your words to describe it. Tell yourself, *Be here now, Travis. It is a beautiful place to be.* You may feel silly at first, but I promise you, it quiets the mind and helps give you mental and emotional energy to deal with whatever challenges you have before you.

- **Be well**. Most people practice being well only when they are not anymore. A lot of us tend to wait until things are falling apart around us before we show them care. That is very true for trauma survivors who struggle with feeling self-care as a selfish act they do not deserve. Many of us will take better care of others or even our cars than of ourselves. You keep your car well by checking the tires, getting the oil changed, and getting the engine checked out. Do the same for yourself. Don't wait until all your lug nuts are loose and the wheels of your life are about to fall off. Remember, self-care is not selfish.

Embracing Light

- Look before you leap. Be sure the next lily pad you are jumping onto is leading you toward your goals (i.e., your best self and not further into bondage).

- *Always* and *never* are never always true. Let go of terminal language.

- Avoid *would've, could've, should've,* and *what-if.* Let go of time-travel language. You will find freedom, healing, and growth in your present, your right now.

- You cannot go back and change your past, but you can bring it into your present and learn from it so that you can change yourself now.

- Be still. Be here. Be well. Make these daily habits.

8

VALUE

Healing the Way We Believe

Do the thing you fear most, and the death of fear is certain.
—Mark Twain

Can we skip this chapter? Kidding/not kidding. Writing about self-belief is still hard. It is harder than sharing the realities of my story in Part One. Even healed, old monsters try to whisper to me, *are you sure you are worthy enough to be believed in*? And I must answer, *yes! I am worthy. I believe in myself.*

I have learned that it's possible to wrestle with doubts about something, and it can still be true. We are not perfect. I do not perfectly believe in myself to this day, but I believe in myself more today than I did yesterday, and I will repeat that tomorrow and until the day I breathe my last. I am convinced there is no such thing as unbelief. For instance: Someone says they do not believe there is a God. I would argue they do not have "unbelief" but an alternative belief. They probably believe, instead, in a universe with a random origin and no intelligent designer behind the scenes. I'm not trying to split hairs, here; this is an important concept. This

101

realization helped me so much in my healing. For so long, I agonized over why I was stuck and could not believe in my worth or in the life I deserved. I remember asking myself, *why are you under the control of so much unbelief?* Then it hit me: I wasn't. I was buried beneath a deep belief, a belief that I was broken, worthless, and destined to live in pain all my life. Unbelief was never my problem; belief in the wrong thing was. I imagine some of you can identify.

Why Is It So Hard to Change?

You do not have to look very far to see people who are savagely committed to their beliefs. Whether it be social media or politics (don't worry, we're not going there), you can find people that will defend their beliefs almost to the point of death, no matter how much they may be challenged or considered wrong by everyone else. It is hilarious, or *sad* may be a better word, to see what hill of belief some people will choose to die on, so to speak.

But, as I look at belief in those arenas, I turn and look in the mirror of my own journey and think, *why could you not see how ludicrous it was to believe in those things?* There must have been something deeper at work. And, of course, there was. Belief is putting trust, faith, or confidence in something or someone. Belief represents our world as we see it, however true or idealized it may be. When I began studying belief, it was discouraging. I thought, *Great, everything I struggle with—trust, faith, and confidence—are the things required for me to believe in myself.* But I so wanted to. Friends and family encouraged me to believe in my potential, in my healing. I read books about it, heard songs about it, and found Scripture to support the need for it. There was going to be no quitting until I believed in the truth of who I really was. I knew I deserved it, and I knew it was necessary for me to grow and move forward.

But only knowing something rarely elicits action; action requires belief. *Oh, great,* you're thinking. *To believe in myself, I must first believe that I deserve to believe in myself.* That's quite comical. Hear me out. Our brains look for patterns around us—in our experiences, culture, and internal narrative. Our beliefs emerge from those patterns. The sun rises every morning, so I believe the sun will rise today. But here is where it gets interesting. When our beliefs are challenged, parts of our brain will come to their defense; the brain doesn't change its beliefs very easily.[8]

So, my brain noticed the patterns of my belief in my worthlessness. Fear and shame became stalwart partners in my daily life. I was entrenched in my trauma narrative and limiting beliefs. When I tried to attack the darkness with the light and the lies with the truth, my monsters came to my defense. They chimed in, *no; you are worthless and unlovable, but that is okay. We got you. We are going to protect you from the scary real world. Just stay comfortable within the walls we have erected for you, and you will be safe.* Wow, it sounds even crazier when I write it down, but I know there are some readers who have emerged from trauma struggles or are still battling them and can fully relate.

Keep fighting it, friends. You are worthy. You have value because you are you. Remember that the monsters, the walls, and all the scary things were created by your own narrative and hacked beliefs. They only have the power you give them. So, take that power back. Speak the truth and the light into your darkness.

Treat Yourself

Most everyone has heard the Bible verse that says to treat others the way you want to be treated (Luke 6:31; Matt. 6:12). For me, that was never a struggle. As with many trauma survivors, the battle is to treat oneself the way we treat others. Now, I have made my share of mistakes. I have learned every lesson in life the hard way, and it still hurts my heart to know that I have hurt people along the way. But other than the pain my poor choices caused; I have never had an issue with loving others. I have, though, had a significant issue with loving myself. God and I wrestled a lot through my journey to freedom. He is good like that. We can bring our pain, brokenness, and raw emotions to Him, and He will love us through it. There were times I wanted God to just let me hate myself. He gives us the freedom to choose, but I kept getting images of how He loves us, and how He had given me the opportunity to love others all over the world by meeting them at the point of their needs. Through that, He broke my heart for my own heart. Make sense?

I remember the day God and I were having one of those wrestling matches that led to clarity. He helped me to look past my abuse, through my poor choices, and into the soul of who He created me to be. This was another of those times that I could almost hear his voice speaking to me, *my child, I love you. I love you enough not to look past your sins, but to pick them up and use them for your good. All you must do is believe in that. Have I not loved others through you that were in pain, in the bondage of sin, stuck at the point of their greatest mistake? Have you not witnessed the chains of bondage broken in others? Who are you that I would not do the same for you? Know this and take it to heart: mercy receives, redemption changes, and grace illuminates.*

Real talk: I do still struggle to believe in myself some days. But I recognize this as a feeling, not who I really am. It is always because I am stressed, tired, or lacking focus, but it is never true. I have given God my bad, my brokenness, my mistakes, and He has brought good out of them all. No matter how far your life gets away from God and His perfect plan for you, He is always only one step away. Nowadays, I feel like a kid on Christmas Eve every night I go to bed. I look forward to waking up and seeing what life has to offer.

Let's Get Ready to Rumble

I am excited that we are almost at Part Three in this book. That is where we will talk about eight personal growth mindsets. I like to call them the eight streams of flow. Flow is about three things: an energized focus, full involvement, and enjoyment in the moment.[9] Before we dive into that, let's glance back at where we have come from. I pray you have gained something from these first eight chapters that has led, or is leading you, to a newfound awareness, freedom, and belief in yourself.

- Belief in yourself is key to freedom, healing, and growth. If you struggle with it, get help. And remember, you can believe for the moment you are in and then keep repeating that.

- Words create worlds. Be intentional about knowing the worlds you are creating.

- Help is not a bad, four-letter word.

- Hate *is* a bad, four-letter word.

- Work to discover your internal narrative. You are writing it every second of your life. Remember, we write our stories (with God's guidance), or our stories write us.

- Fear is a construct of our words and beliefs. Much of the freedom we seek is hidden behind a core fear. Ask yourself, what do I fear most in life? The answer to that likely points the way to the work you must do to find your best self.

- Self-care is never selfish.

- Pain refines; it doesn't define. Do not fear pain. It is trying to tell you where some work needs to be done in your life.

- IIWII – It is what it is. Sometimes that is all we can say to hold ourselves in the moment, holding on to only the things we can control.

- Vulnerability is not a weakness, it is the strength that will guide you into healthier relationships, more peace, and finding the real you.

- Speak about your thoughts and feelings intentionally. Is it true? Is it happening now? Does it have value to teach me something and move me forward?

- Complaining is pointless. It is like trying to dip water with a fishnet.

- Feelings are feelings, period. They are not facts. They are not who you are.

- Your internal dialogue will determine your external direction.

- Learn before you leap. Do not end up like the frog in the alligator's mouth.

- *Always* and *never* are never always true.

- Be aware of using terminal and time-travel language. It will rob you of energy, peace, and focus.

Embracing Light

- Be brave. Courage and being afraid can coexist. Believe in yourself for this moment and then keep repeating. That is bravery. Courage is not being fearless; it is never giving up.

- Do the thing you fear, and fear will die. Step into the painful narrative. You wrote it and believed in it. That is powerful. Now, just reclaim that power for good.

- Ask yourself, *does my internal belief system move me forward or hold me in bondage?* Challenge every belief that does not teach you, grow you, and move you forward.

- Be real with yourself. Embrace vulnerability.

- Love yourself. Do not wait for you to feel like things are perfect to show yourself some love. Are those you love always perfect? No. But you still love them. Do the same for you.

- Embrace your story. Embrace your moments. Work today to be a better version of yourself than you were yesterday. Plan and take your best next step, then repeat.

PART THREE

Reimagining
Your Future

Expectancy: the feeling that something exciting or pleasant is about to happen. Expectancy is about making an intimate connection with yourself as we embrace the things that truly bring us to life. Here we explore eight practical and life-altering mindsets that will allow us to embrace a new, healthy experience of belief and being.

Hunger—Embracing flow in craving
Thankfulness—Embracing flow in contentment
Awe—Embracing flow in centeredness
Wrestling—Embracing flow in conquest
Intimacy—Embracing flow in compassion
Symphony—Embracing flow in community
Dance—Embracing flow in connection
Story—Embracing flow in creation

So, why did I choose these eight words? They came to me when I was searching to make sense of life after losing my dad, far too young, in a battle with cancer. I felt like they were God-inspired, but I didn't know what to do with them at that moment. I set them aside for years, but they resurfaced as I began to write my story. Now I see they are all a perfect example of the legacy my dad left me through living his life. Little did he know how they would become the impetus for me to know myself in ways I never thought possible. I like to call them the eight streams of flow.

Why do I call it flow? In positive psychology, flow is the idea of being completely immersed in the experience of energized focus or clarity, joy in the moment, and being fully present. Think of it as being "in the zone." I used to wonder if that was something I would ever experience. Thankfully, I learned it was what I was created for all along.

How would you be different if you could embrace your moments with joy, presence, and peace? Step into your light and discover your full potential to experience the life you desire.

9

HUNGER

Embracing Flow in Craving

Don't try to add more years to your life.
Better add more life to your years.
—Blaise Pascal

*H*unger—a strong desire or craving for something
When we hear the word *hunger*, most people think of
growling bellies followed by the voices in our heads
screaming for us to eat. But our hearts hunger for things like
love and connection, our minds for things like knowledge
and peace, and our souls for meaning and purpose. As in our
hunger for food, all these areas of desire and craving have the
potential for both good and bad outcomes, depending on
how we satisfy them. As the saying goes, we are what we eat.

Choose Wisely

You are moving along through your day, and then you get
that gnawing pain in your belly. The voice in your head says,
"Feed me!" Now your thoughts turn to the question of what
you currently desire or crave. It could be a thick, juicy steak, a

111

healthy salad, or you may just want to stuff your face quickly, with no regard for health or calories, and order a fast-food meal. On the surface, we make our decisions based on practical things like what is available, convenient, and fits well into our schedule. But then we are faced with the deeper and more entrenched ideals of whether our choices are good for us and fit into our long-term health goals. Any number of choices might fill our immediate need to satiate our hunger, but unless we choose mindfully, we may experience more harm than good. Choosing what is fast and easy gets us back to what we were doing quickly, but it could add inches to our waistlines and bring us health challenges. Making more intentional and mindful choices takes time and effort, but it can bring us a sense of self-satisfaction and help us maintain good health. That which is true for physical hunger is also true for the hunger we experience in our hearts, minds, and souls. How halfhearted or intentional we are with satisfying hunger in these areas will determine if we live our lives in the peace and calm of flow or the pain and dysfunction of chaos. In my journey, I have learned there are three areas we need to master to embrace flow in the daily cravings of our lives: desire, expectation, and satisfaction.

All the choices we face are made according to both conscious and unconscious sets of directions or instructions. Like most, I was always aware of my conscious thoughts. I may have wrestled with them, sometimes making better choices than others, but I was always aware of the internal dialogue. Our unconscious narrative is not as easy to grasp. We must know what we are looking for and we must instruct our brains (ourselves) to call the desired information up into our consciousness. It is something that must be developed into a habit. We have already discussed in the first two parts of this book how to raise awareness to that hidden narrative and how to find freedom and healing, but that process, once learned, is something we must embrace for the rest of our lives. We humans are dynamic and ever-changing, so practicing these new habits will help us stay on the path to freedom and growth, no matter what we may face.

The process of discovering and embracing these eight mindsets or streams of flow was both humbling and empowering. It was amazing to witness the changes in the way I thought, felt, and faced challenges in my daily life. It would have been easy to stay stuck and broken over my old ways, but I was too excited and encouraged in my experience with the new ways of thinking. I remember being aware, during my brokenness, that I would have times I hungered for the chaos. As I connected to the way I saw myself, I could see there were times I desired the attacks from the monsters of shame and worthlessness because they supported my expectations of what I deserved in life. There was more satisfaction or fulfillment in the internal battles than there was in what I saw as the temporary and fleeting experiences of peace and calm. You must be careful what you hunger for because you just might get exactly what you wanted.

The Fire in Our Soul

Desire is not something that is inherently bad. It is natural. We are wired to desire food and water to sustain life. We are wired to desire love, connection, and community. Money, fame, and power are also not inherently bad in and of themselves. Desire itself is not bad, but what and how we desire sometimes can be. All the things we listed can be bad for us. There is such a thing as too much food, too much water, and too much money, power, or fame. When the pursuit of fulfilling these desires gets out of hand, we have obesity, addictions, chaos, and more.

Four of the seven deadly sins are about having a disordered desire (envy, gluttony, greed, and lust).[10] They can fulfill us, and they can overfill us. We can also have too little desire. In the short term that can bring about boredom and laziness. In the long term, a lack of desire can bring depression and hopelessness. The broadness of our desires affects the way we live our lives. Someone with too many different desires can be seen as unfocused and never satisfied. That describes a lot of the years of my bondage to my trauma narrative. I bounced from one opportunity to another and never stayed focused on one project too long. I know it bothered some people around me. If I am honest, it would have bothered me, too.

My dad used to ask me, "Why can't you stick to one thing and be the very best at it?" I didn't know the answer when he was still alive. If he were still here, I'd say, "Dad, I felt too worthless to try to be the best at anything, to stay focused on one thing for very long. My desires were never satisfied by those things because I desired something the world alone could not give me: peace and calm in the chaos of my thoughts."

My old self was caught up in trying to quench too many different desires. I was also too primal in the pursuit of fulfilling them. What I mean is, I was on autopilot. My unconscious thoughts were telling me what I wanted without me even being consciously aware of it. If anyone would have stopped me and asked what I was all about, what I was hoping to accomplish in my life through my thoughts and actions, I am not sure I would have had a clear message. Come to think of it, I am reminded as I write this that people did ask me; I just didn't appreciate the importance of the question. I remember being all over the place with my responses. I did not know the source of my desires, and I was clueless about how to truly fulfill them. So, how did I move from having my desires fuel my chaotic and hacked internal narrative to the peace and calm of being in the flow with my cravings?

I realized three truths about my desires, and I discovered three questions to ask myself that centered me in the flow that my soul longed for. Here are the three truths

- Desire, like so many things, is driven by our own narrative.

- Desire needs a purpose and focus to have clarity on how to fulfill it.

- Desire sustains us as humans. If that is true, then knowing ourselves better would help us better understand our desires.

The three questions I asked are the following:

- **Who are you?** That is one of the hardest questions we ever face. When I experienced healing in my narrative, that was the first question that popped into my head. I thought, *okay, Travis, you have freedom from the pain and bondage. You say you are free. So, who are you now?* I sat there, like most people, vapor locked. I had the answers most of us give, such as what I do for a living, my career positions, and my family roles. But who am I? It helped me to answer this question with a question. Who am I *not*? That answer was much easier. I experienced that revelation as I worked to bring my darkness into the light of truth. There were a lot of things I allowed to define me, that I discovered were lies of my own making. I listed out everything that I knew in my heart that was not the real me. Some lies were hard to let go of; I had believed them so long they had become an enigma: pleasant in some ways and unbearable in others. You try it. It might be best done with a trusted friend, coach, or counselor—someone to help you see the truth of who you are.

- **What ignites your passion?** I was passionate about a lot of things. I could get excited about anything that helped others. But being passionate kept me living in chaos and bouncing from one thing to another. I was passionate about things without knowing what my own personal true passion was. Passion is that one thing that stirs us, that brings us to life. My publisher, Kary Oberbrunner, helps us discover our passion by posing a question: "What makes you a soul on fire?" I wrestled with that for quite a while. What truly ignites my soul? And then it came to me. My passion is to help others master their internal narratives so they can know the freedom to pursue what sets their souls on fire and embrace their best lives. That was it. It stirs my soul just to write it down. This was my if you were king for a day, what I would you do?" statement. We all have this within us. We are wired for passion. As we seek to find our true selves, we find passion at the intersection of our gifts, talents, and abilities.

I love the discipline of forcing our passion statement into one sentence. If you look at all the great people in history, the ones that truly changed the world, they each had a singular focus on a singular passion that ignited their soul. I see a trend in our culture of a lot of people being afraid to focus truly on their one passion. I believe social media has entrenched us in a fear we are going to miss something if we are too focused. What are you passionate about? What sets your soul on fire? Whether it becomes a career or just the pursuit of your life, living out your passion will bring you alive more than anything else. It will connect your soul to meaning and purpose.

- **Does the fulfillment of your desires sustain you to pursue your passion, or does it hinder you?** This question helps bring clarity in all areas of desire, whether it be the body, heart, soul, or mind. Think about it. Does my meal choice today sustain my body and give me energy to pursue my passion, or does it hinder it? Does my desire to connect to this person sustain the pursuit of my passion or does it hinder it? This one question was paradigm-shifting in helping me develop clarity, focus, and intention in the pursuit and healthy fulfillment of my desires.

That Other Reality

We talked about our realities in the chapter on healing our internal voice. We have the actual reality around us, our believed reality about ourselves, and our desired reality or expectations. For us to experience the peace and calm of flow, our three realities must be as closely in sync with one another as possible. Living with anxiety or in bondage to the hacked narrative of our past traumas will usually lead us to put too much emphasis on our expectations. We either expect the real world around us to match them perfectly, or we have chaos. This can manifest in frustration and anger with others or ourselves. This is what kept me steeped in shame and hating myself. I could never meet my own expectations. That hindered me from having enough courage to break free from the bondage and believing I deserved freedom.

So, how do we align our expectations with our daily realities so they can support the pursuit of flow in satisfying our hunger? Here are the three questions I used to refine the process:

- Are your expectations a guide leading you through your daily life, or are you expecting the actual reality around you to give into and fit your desired reality? We cannot put too much emphasis on our expectations and forget we only control two things in life: our own choices and how we respond to everyone else's choices. Your expectations must remain flexible, dynamic, and adaptable to your world of experience. If not, you will live or die on the hill of whether your expectations manifested perfectly in your real life.

- *Are your expectations supporting a positive belief in yourself?* Before my healing, my expectations told me I would always be worthless and never fully loved by anyone. That is the opposite of experiencing flow. You cannot know the peace and calm that flow brings when you have chaos. So, you must always hold your expectations accountable for maintaining a positive attitude and belief in yourself. Otherwise, your intentions for good will always be in a battle with your negative voice that expects all things to be bad.

- *Are your expectations sustaining you in the pursuit of your passion or hindering it?* Yes, I am repeating that question. It is one we should ask ourselves constantly, especially while engaging in each of the eight stages of flow in our lives.

The Art of Staying Filled

We have discussed desire and expectation, and now the last area of focus to help us experience flow in our cravings is satisfaction. Staying filled. Being satisfied. Looking back at the most primal of our cravings for food, satisfaction can be seen to exist at every level of choice. The person who chose the fast-food meal, the one with the healthy salad, or the one taking the time to prepare a home-cooked steak with all the side dishes can each experience satisfaction. So how do we differentiate between satisfaction that is good for us and that which is temporary and fleeting, sometimes even destructive?

Before, satisfaction was something that I constantly pursued but never fully experienced. I want to say I had a satisfaction in my soul through my belief in God, but there was even chaos there. God offered me the fullness of peace and calm, a satisfied soul, but I thought I could only fully receive it when I overcame my own mental health struggles. How untrue I learned that was! Unlike being able to easily fill my belly full and satisfy my physical hunger, I could not seem to do that with my heart, soul, and mind. Why? First, I was not listening well to my internal narrative. In my unconscious, my hacked narrative was supporting the lies that I did not deserve to be satisfied. I could never be satisfied because I would never be worthy or enough. So, no matter how many external efforts I made to be happy and satisfied, the pursuit was unending because of what I call the micro-decisions I was making in my head. These small thoughts—lies, to be more correct—kept me in bondage. I told myself I would never be satisfied until I attained the goals of my hacked narrative, created by six-year-old me: fix the world, make everyone happy, and you have permission to be okay. In so doing, I had created parameters for my satisfaction that were unrealistic (no one can make the whole world smile), unattainable (no one can fix everyone), and unhealthy (hence my poor choices and getting stuck thinking about my worthlessness).

I am so glad I broke free from that bondage. How did I move from there to flow in my cravings? I asked these three questions, like the questions for expectations:

- *Does your pursuit of satisfaction bring you true fulfillment?* You must always question whether your answers are supporting temporary feelings or whether you are truly fulfilled and satisfied.

- *Does your pursuit of satisfaction bring lasting change?* We may be okay choosing Chinese food to satiate our physical hunger and then be hungry again two hours later. But, in matters of the heart, soul, and mind, continuously having to dip back into the well to find satisfaction might signal that we are making poor choices. I constantly had to serve others and be involved in projects to feel satisfied with myself. I had come to depend on them as a substitute for what I felt I could never attain. This was not true satisfaction.

- *Does your pursuit of satisfaction improve your life?* In other words, does your satisfaction meet random, temporary needs, or does it sustain you in the pursuit of your passion that sets your soul on fire?

A fast-food burger is not going to sustain your body for the long haul without some damage. So, too, choosing poorly in our quest for satisfaction can be unhealthy for our heart, soul, and mind. Build a habit of marking the success of your choices with the answers to the questions above. It changed my perspective completely and helped me to find the peace and calm of flow.

Making healthy choices in the pursuit of satisfying our cravings makes all the difference in whether our lives will continue to be a rollercoaster ride between peace and chaos, or one of balance and calm. Being in the flow is all about experiencing an energized focus (clarity), full involvement (presence), and enjoyment for the moment (joy). Work to master the internal narrative that guides you on the fulfillment of cravings in a way that keeps you in the flow you deserve in life.

Embracing Light

- Hunger or craving is more than just your body's need for food and water. Be aware of the cravings of your heart, soul, and mind as well.

- Make conscious and intentional efforts to master your desires, or they will master you.

- What brings you passion? What sets your soul on fire? Do not fear pursuing the answer to those questions. Instead, fear living a life where you never feel the passion.

- Do your choices sustain you in the pursuit of your focus and passion, or do they hinder you?

- Be sure you manage your expectations well. They are meant to be your guides, not your god.

- Pursue flow in all your choices: an energized focus (or clarity), full involvement (or presence), and enjoyment in your moment (or joy).

10

THANKFULNESS

Embracing Flow in Contentment

Piglet noticed that even though he had a Very Small Heart,
it could hold a rather large amount of Gratitude.
—*A.A. Milne, Winnie the Pooh*

You may read this chapter's title and think, "What does thankfulness have to do with hacked narratives and trauma recovery?" Everything. I have the firm belief, after my own journey, that you cannot fully recover from any kind of pain or trauma without being able to find contentment again. Contentment, in our heart, mind, and soul, is completely antithetical to chaos. I lived forty years with the struggle of working to carve out a joyful life for me and my family while my mind was a place of utter chaos. It was like walking through life not knowing when you were going to step on the next land mine that would send your thoughts, feelings, and emotions into a tailspin of pain and negativity. Rediscovering my ability to experience true contentment helped me to break free from that chaos of lies and limiting beliefs. Contentment worked to defuse the landmines so I could find my true self.

These four practical mindsets of thankfulness helped me find the peace and calm of flow in contentment.

The Most Important Place on The Planet

It was August 2010. Dad had endured a rough four months of treatment for his cancer, but this was a good month. He had gotten some of his strength back. He was the Pop that everyone knew and loved. August was special because he had the ability to do two things that he loved most, build a wheelchair ramp for someone in need with his best friend, Marshall, and go fishing with me. We arrived at one of our favorite fishing holes, grabbed our equipment, and headed for the boat that was always there waiting for us. I could tell some things were harder for my dad. Navigating the uneasy terrain and getting into the boat revealed the price his body had paid for ninety days of cancer treatment. But my dad was there; he was present. It was a great day. The weather cooperated, and we started catching fish the moment we put our hooks in the water. I promised myself I wasn't going to bring up anything negative to do with his treatment or cancer. But he chose to. Dad turned to me.

"You know how everyone thinks I am taking all of this so well? Well, for one, the truth is it's hard. It hurts. But two, what looks like me taking all of this in stride is really me learning to be content in all things. No matter what happens from here, I have joy in the life I have lived. I am fully content and at peace." Okay, I was trying to enjoy fishing without crying, but he sure was making it hard.

"Dad, you know you are the one who taught me to embrace my moments. I know you always hear me telling people to be present, to be here now. Well, that was you. That is part of your legacy to me and the rest of the family." He smiled that crooked, million-dollar smile I remember seeing for the first time when I was six years old, and then he put a different bait on his line.

"Don't forget the most important part", he said, "the contentment. A lot of people are present in their moments, but they are present with their frustration, anger, fears, and hate. The key to a happy life is knowing how to be in the moment and be content with it. Then you just keep repeating that."

Right there, I felt he was speaking directly to me and telling me he had recognized my struggles in life, which I thought I had hidden well. He was leaving me with that bit of wisdom in case things didn't turn out well for him. I always wanted to tell my dad about my struggles, about the sexual abuse, but I just never found the courage. It was never because I didn't trust him, but I didn't trust myself to be worthy of burdening anyone with all that pain. We enjoyed ourselves that day. We caught nineteen fish between the two of us. It was a great reminder that the most important place on the planet is where you are, the moment you are in, the people you are with, and with a heart of contentment. August 2010 was the month I cherished most that year. After that, he endured a month of surgery and recovery, another month of rehab, and then he was gone.

Road Work

Our brains are one magnificent, powerful, and mystery-filled organ. Every moment of our lives, we are writing our stories. Every thought, feeling, emotion, and experience are logged, and we never run out of memory. At the biological level, every time we have an experience, it either creates a new neural pathway, or road, in our brains or lights up an existing one from a previous, similar experience.[11] I learned the true power of our brains during my journey to freedom from the pain and hacked narratives of my trauma story. It is equally powerful in the good things as it is in the bad things. I am no neuroscientist, but here is my view of how my trauma brain worked: All our experiences exist on these neural pathways our brain creates, and for those things we think about or experience more often than others, those neural pathways become like superhighways.

My brain was carved with several negative neural super-highways, including my feelings of worthlessness, the painful memory of sexual abuse, and the thoughts that went through my head when I felt I let people down. This gets people stuck in their trauma narrative. Those destructive and unhealthy superhighways become the automatic pathway for our thoughts and feelings. Life can go well, and then someone says something. It makes you feel sad, but not just any kind of sad. It is that same experience of sadness when you were being abused. So now, that current feeling awakens the whole trauma experience of your past. That neural pathway is strengthened and widened. Every sad feeling like your feelings during the trauma reawakens the pain, fear, and shame of your past. And this is true for every negative cognition we hold in our brains from past trauma and painful experiences. No wonder that hamster on the narrative wheel goes crazy sometimes.

For those that have struggled with this, or are still struggling through it, I know it can be hard to overcome. It can be even harder to help those around you understand what you are going through if they have never experienced it. They may even think you are crazy. I thought that about myself at times. But here's the deal: if the brain remembers everything and is that powerful, and if my narrative or beliefs about my story put me in that depth of bondage, then my brain is equally strong to set me free.

This is where thankfulness comes in. Chaos cannot coexist where contentment is present. We may bounce back and forth between the two, but we cannot exist in both states at once. The more we nurture those neural pathways of thankfulness and contentment, the less we fire up the ones filled with negative and painful things. Think about things that make you feel thankful. Dwell on thoughts that stir joy. That gives you the strength to wrestle with the painful things you want to defeat. You have what it takes to overcome your negative narrative with a positive one. Thankfulness is key to finding that sweet spot of flow and the balance and peace that moves you forward in pursuit of passion and wholeness in life.

Three Things

This is one of the simplest practices I implore clients to undertake in their own individual journeys of freedom, healing, and growth. While simple, it carries the potential to change everything about how you think, act, and feel. And what is this simple, yet profound task? Be intentionally thankful every day. This is not just having an attitude of thankfulness or a heart of thankfulness. Those are important, but this is actively thinking and speaking about what you are thankful for. Why three things? Well, my brain always learns and remembers things in triads, and this is just how I did it on my own journey. In my experience, the three things also helped cement the habit and foster self-accountability. I wouldn't let myself just speak one or two, but I also would not pour out a long list of things, thinking it would give me a pass for a few days. Habit came with repetition, and repetition helped strengthen those strong positive neural pathways. I noticed this helped me in all aspects of my healing from a life of negativity and limiting beliefs.

What are you thankful for today? Name three things and contemplate why you are thankful for them. Think outside the box. As a matter of fact, burn any box you find yourself in. See with your soul and all five senses, not just your eyes. There are things to be thankful for everywhere.

Nourish The System

I remember the day my wife, Regenea, and I were working with a client through her trauma narrative from marital struggles. We were sharing our story with the young lady when my wife uttered the words that shook me to my core with joy and thankfulness. They were not new words. She had said them to me before. It was just amazing to hear them spoken to someone else. It was amazing to witness so much light coming from the darkness we had endured and overcome. She looked at the client and said, "No one would want to *willingly* experience what Travis and I have, but I am thankful for all we have endured because it has brought us to this place of growth. It freed him from his past trauma, and it has set us on a path of joy and peace."

All of that came about because both of us were able to help each other experience our path with a heart of thankfulness. Thankfulness, when practiced intentionally as a habit, can spread throughout everything in our lives. And that is what we want it to do. We want the contentment that comes from a thankful heart to permeate and nourish the whole system that is our heart, soul, and mind.

Remember the seed factory we talked about earlier? Our internal narratives (or the words we tell ourselves) are like seeds that produce and nurture our thoughts and feelings. Our internal dialogue determines our external direction. If we sow seeds of pain, fear, and limiting beliefs, that is what our life will look like. I struggled with growing all these things in the garden that was my life for far too long. As soon as I understood this concept, I found the power by speaking truth into my own life and by speaking joy and thankfulness over all things. Did you read what I said, *all things*? Almost all of us have painful experiences in our past. Some of us have experienced great traumas. The power of thankfulness becomes a superpower when we can find things to be thankful for, even in our darkest times.

I am not just serving you up empty thoughts to inspire or encourage you. I am speaking the truth. A lot of things in my past hurt. I was greatly damaged by the sexual abuse I endured. I hurt others in my struggles with addictions and poor choices. I hurt my wife and family deeply in the worst of those poor choices. And I have come to the place of growth that I can honestly say we have found thankfulness for it all. What other options do I have? I could wallow in the pain of regret and unforgiveness, or I could choose joy and thankfulness. I chose the latter, and it changed my life. I took God up on the promise he speaks about in the book of Romans. He tells us He will use *all* things for good if we only believe (Romans 8:28). And he has done that for me, and more.

I am thankful for my story. I find thankfulness in the dark days of my sexual abuse because I can now help others through similar struggles, particularly other men. I know the journey from the bondage of a deeply hacked trauma narrative to freedom. I am thankful that God has taken all my mistakes and poor choices and turned them over for good to help others. Thankfulness brought me contentment for the moment, and I have learned how to string those moments together for a life of joy, peace, and love. Living life in the flow of contentment is one of the most powerful choices you can make. Dwell often on the question, "What am I thankful for?"

Embracing Light

- Wherever you are, be all there. Be fully present with your moments and strive to find contentment in each moment you experience. It will make all the difference in your life.

- Chaos cannot coexist with contentment. Choose to be thankful. Bathing your heart in contentment can help give you the mental and emotional strength to rid your life of any chaos that exists.

- Every day, identify three things you are thankful for. Think about them. Name them out loud. Journal about them. Start with a goal of doing this for thirty days. Building intentional thankfulness into your everyday life can completely change the way you think, act, and feel.

- Believe in the power of contentment in every area of your life. Actively sowing seeds of thankfulness help to nourish the heart, mind, and soul with the power of positivity. Negativity is a habit shared by many who have experienced trauma. The good news is that positivity can be equally habit forming, and it starts with a thankful heart.

- Can you identify things to be thankful for, even in the darkest parts of your trauma narrative or painful past experiences? Being able to do this gave me a fresh perspective on the bondage I was in and gave me the strength to challenge my monsters and defeat my limiting beliefs.

11

AWE

Embracing Flow in Centeredness

Collect moments, not things. You will
discover more peace and joy
and will never need to rent a storage unit.
—Travis White

We have become a culture of people who are not easily awed. As a matter of fact, I talk to a lot of people who do not even have a clear understanding of what the word means. Even fewer folks understand how awe can help make your mind and body healthier.

What is awe? In my own words, it is a sense of reverential wonder. It is a feeling of being mesmerized, mind-blown, and caught up in the present moment of the experience. We can be awed by something by surprise, and we can intentionally focus our attention on things in ways to bring about awe. I cannot view the night sky without getting that feeling. The beauty and vastness still my mind. Time seems to slow as I enjoy staring out into the universe. I am more aware of myself and more present with my thoughts and feelings.

This illustrates how awe can be healthy for us. It slows us down. It sharpens our focus on the present moment. Awe helps to center us or bring us into a state of mindfulness. Too many of us live our lives off-center and anything but mindful because of busyness, responsibilities, our desire for more stuff, competition with others, trauma, you name it. Countless things rob us of the beauty of life that is all around us.

Let me take a moment to discuss mindfulness. Ten years ago, that was an obscure term in America. Many people still do not understand what it means, even though it has become the latest cliché word being thrown around in self-care circles. Simply put, mindfulness means to be aware of oneself in the present moment.

How do awe, centeredness, and mindfulness work together to improve our lives? Awe stops us and brings us into the present moment. It is one of many things that can bring about a state of mindfulness. Remember, I said we can intentionally invite ourselves into moments of awe. Once a day, I try to stop and observe something around me until it brings me into that space. Maybe it means watching a squirrel eat corn in our front yard or studying the intricacies of a flower.

Okay, I probably lost some of you there, especially some of you men. I can hear one of my buddies now, saying, "Wow, Travis, you are getting all up in your feels with the squirrels and flowers. I am not sure that would help me in any way." Well, haters are going to hate, but I can tell you this: since I started practicing mindfulness and intentionally finding things to bring about the experience of awe, I am more relaxed, less stressed, and calmer. My blood pressure is better, and I have tons more joy in life. In other words, I am living life more centered. I highly recommend it. In today's hurried world, more people have *awful* experiences rather than *awe*-full ones. Those who have dealt with past trauma and mental health issues like anxiety and depression struggle, even more, to stay centered. I remember the chaos of my hacked narrative and the negative things I believed about life and myself. There were years at a time where I could not calm my mind at all. Mindfulness, for trauma survivors, feels like something a million miles away, but I learned the path for getting there was the belief that I could get there, the belief that I deserved that peace and calm. It is a process. It takes time and dedication. Having been on both sides of the fence between chaos and centeredness, my advice is to do whatever it takes to get over to the centered side. You deserve it.

Listening, the Cliffs, and the Old Man

I first studied mindfulness in grad school. I believed in its power to help, particularly for trauma survivors and those dealing with anxiety and PTSD. I taught it to several clients with great success. But truth be told, I was never purely sold on it, especially for helping me in my bondage, until a family trip to Ireland. In 2012, two years after my father passed away, my mom, wife, our two children, and I decided to chase our lifelong dream of seeing Ireland. Dad had always wanted to see it, so this was a sort of homage to him, and we all needed some healing. We were pinning high hopes on the Emerald Isle to deliver. I did not have set plans for what I wanted to see happen; I just wanted to experience something in a way to get closer to finding myself. I was very depressed over the loss of my father, and that pushed my negative, self-hate-filled trauma narrative right to the surface. I was not in a good place. But, as I did most of my life, I put on a smile and went forward. The monsters nodded in approval. *That's right, put on a strong front, Travis. We'll stay down here and torture you with your worthlessness from your safe prison of fear and shame.*

The tour bus pulled into the town of Kilkenny. It did not disappoint. The people were all kind, and the food was amazing. The last place we toured was the old church in the city center. It was ornate, yet simple, and a reverent quietness filled the air. I was walking around the sanctuary, alone with my thoughts, and straight into an unexpected moment of awe. An old man—a town local, no doubt—was sitting in a dimly lit corner of the church, near the altar. At first glance, he looked to be catching a nap, but then he cracked a little smile. He was lost in the most beautiful moment of mindfulness I have ever witnessed. You could tell he was aware of every sound around him, every whispering voice, and when he took a deep breath, he had this pleasant look on his face, as if he was smelling his grandmother's freshly baked brown bread. I just stood there, lost in the moment. My soul longed to know that kind of peace.

After about fifteen minutes, he opened his eyes, and they connected to mine. I took the liberty of going over to say hello. He invited me to sit down. He told me his family had lived in Kilkenny for six generations. I had to speak.

"If you don't mind me inquiring, what were you doing all this time sitting here? Whatever it was, I can tell you, just watching you brought a sense of calm to my soul." He smiled and shared,

"My family has attended church here ever since our people moved here. I come here every day to listen. I listen to God, and to my own thoughts. Life can get crazy, and I need this time to tend to my own peace so that I do not get lost in all that crazy."

What a beautiful experience in seeing the value of practicing mindfulness and being sure we are staying centered. This man will never know it, but he played a pivotal role in my being able to eventually face down my monsters and attack the pain and chaos with a centered and peaceful mind.

If that wasn't enough, the next day we toured the Cliffs of Moher. There is no way I can find the words here to describe the beauty of the grassy rolling hills, the steep jagged cliffs, and the beautiful view of the ocean. I sat in the tall grass overlooking the cliffs and worked hard to channel the spirit of my new friend from Kilkenny. I breathed in the salty Irish air with great intention. I cleared my mind, working hard to just be present. No agenda. Just to listen. I made peace with the loss of my father that day. Oh, I still have moments of sadness over his loss, but my soul is at peace in knowing he lived a full life and left a grand legacy to his family. I want to say I was able to slay my monsters on those cliffs, but that would not be true. What I did, however, was to discover I had more power than I thought to quiet them, if even for a few moments. What I learned there that day would serve me well in my journey to freedom and healing. Slow down, friends. Listen. You don't have to be at a church in Kilkenny or on the sheer cliffs of Western Ireland. Just be present, wherever you are. Spend a few minutes a day to do as the old man in the church: refocus, recenter, and be sure you are still in touch with your true self. If you cannot accomplish this on your own, find someone to help guide you. Your peace depends on it, and your soul hungers for it.

Mindful or Mind-full

The picture is the same for most Americans: Rush through life working, paying bills, buying more things and toys, and running on empty. On top of that, most of us do it with phones in our faces, televisions in every room of the house, and a constant case of fatigue. Social media is filled with working-for-the-weekend attitudes. If we can just make it to Friday, we can recharge and be ready for Monday. How does that work for most people? Not very well. Do you know what working for the weekend gets you? You end up wasting 72 percent of your life while looking forward to living the other 28 percent of it. And what does this mentality get us as a country? We lead the world in suicides, divorce, use of psychotropic medications, and mental health diagnoses. Our minds are full, but we desperately need to experience being mindful. Remember, no matter how fast you rush through life, no matter your economic status, we all have the same 168 hours a week to make a difference in this world.

For trauma survivors and others dealing with mental health issues, I get why you might live this kind of life. I did it for a long time. The busier we stay and the more focused we are on others and other things, the more we drown out the monsters inside. If we rush through life and keep our minds full of stuff, we won't have to hear their voices reminding us we are not enough, that we're failures, worthless, unlovable.

It does not work. I tried it in every way possible, chasing career goals, leading projects to help others, helping clients find the freedom I believed I did not deserve. None of it slew the monsters of my hacked internal narrative. Do you know what finally did? I learned to listen to that narrative and not fear it. Also, I learned that I deserved peace, and not all the chaos that came from the lies I birthed and believed about myself. Trauma changes the brain, but so does mindfulness. I found the courage to connect to my unconscious thoughts, where the monsters of my trauma resided and doled out their lies about my worth and value. I took deep breaths, and I spoke the truth into the lies; I shined the light into my darkness. I recognized the hacked narrative, reassessed what was true and what was lying, and I rebooted how I saw myself.

What were my primary tools? Listening and breathing were especially helpful. You need to do the work to discover the power of breathing as a part of your mindfulness routine. Intentional and relaxed breathing calms the stress response in our bodies, pushes out the feel-good hormones like serotonin, and quiets our minds so that we can focus on the moment. No, it won't happen overnight for you. It takes belief in yourself, practice, and repetition. It makes sense that breathing helps to center us on our inner selves so well; it is the first thing we do in this life, and it is the last. Be present with yourself and make all those breaths in between count.

Consider Your Ways

The book of Haggai in the Hebrew scriptures is only about two pages long. We can summarize it more briefly still: The prophet Haggai was instructed by God to refocus the Jews on their task at hand: rebuilding the temple. They had moved back into their homeland after being in exile, and life had quickly gotten back to their version of normal. They were caught up in the daily rush of life like so many of us Americans do. God instructed Haggai to challenge the people to consider their ways.[12] If you think about it, God was really calling them into mindfulness, challenging them to center themselves on the moment and what was most important. I want to close this chapter with some bullet-point thoughts to help us consider our ways as we seek to find flow in centeredness and embrace the awe of life around us.

- Be still. Put down the phone and turn off the television regularly and intentionally. Seek to reconnect with your inner self. Challenge negative thoughts.

- Slow down. Treat life as a buffet and not a fast-food drive thru. Enjoy your moments.

- Burn your box. Get outside your box of mindless habits and busyness before the rest of your mind atrophies from lack of use.

- Look up. Open your eyes. Look for things and opportunities to be awed.

- Breathe. Realize the importance and benefit of regular, intentional breathing. Relax. Slow your thoughts. Think of nothing but your breath for two minutes. Breathe in through the nose and out through your mouth, using full-lung breaths.

- Be brave. Ask God to show you the world around you and yourself through His eyes.

- Seek clarity. As you breathe, listen. As you listen, consider your ways. Feed and nourish the positive in your mind like plants in a garden. Pull up all the weeds of negative thoughts. If you still struggle with past trauma, anxiety, or other mental health issues, you may need to seek help with this process. Remember: asking for health is brave.

Embracing Light

- Be awed, with great focus and frequency. Look at the world in ways that stir wonder and occasionally blow your mind. It is good for your heart, mind, soul, and body.

- Listen, most often with no agenda. Invite the world around you to enter your consciousness. Be present and in touch with your surroundings. That will help hone your listening skills and give you strength when you are attacking those negative internal narratives and limiting beliefs.

- Breathe. Realize the power of focused and intentional mindful breathing. One to two times a day will relax you, help you focus better, and help to keep you in that flow.

- Slow down. No matter how fast you move through life, you have 168 hours in a week. Stop working for the weekend, and instead put your energy into embracing your moments, every single one of them.

- Use mindfulness to better embrace your right now, this present moment. That is the only place you can find yourself, pursue freedom and healing, and experience peace and calm. Let go of *was* and *not yet,* or they will rob you of your *now.*

12

WRESTLING

Embracing Flow in Conquest

All we have to decide is what to do
with the time that is given us.
—Gandalf, The Fellowship of the Ring

My dad knew how to wrestle. When he experienced a conquest in his life of any kind, it was most often for all the right reasons. I know I use him in a lot of illustrations, but isn't that what a strong legacy is all about? He wasn't perfect, but he lived simply and with intention. Maybe that is why most of the great life lessons I learned from him were never planned. They just happened while Dad was being Dad.

When our children were young, we all lived on some acreage next door to my parents. It was a beautiful place with rolling pastureland and wooded forests. But it was missing one thing that my dad loved: a pond. We had plenty of friends and neighbors that let us fish in theirs, but he wanted his own. They had just built their home and did not really have the money to pay someone to dig the size pond he wanted, but I learned to never doubt my father when he set his mind to something.

One day, as we all enjoyed Sunday dinner together, my dad made an announcement.

"I have decided I am building the pond myself. It will be about two acres in size and eight to ten feet at its deepest. It is going to be great." I grinned at him.

"You got some heavy equipment around here that we don't know about?" I asked. He looked over at my mom, already shaking her head.

"I am building it with my tractor."

Now, let's set the stage here for how much wrestling this was going to take to make this another famous Max White conquest. Dad had one tractor that we used to care for our fifteen acres of land. It was a 1954 International Harvester Farmall 100. These tractors were built solid as a rock, but he had only two implements to use with it: a brush hog for mowing and a five-foot-wide box blade. A box blade is used to spread material and level ground out. They are not used to dig holes, especially two acres in size and ten feet deep. But the next day, and every day for a solid two months, he was on that tractor moving dirt into a pile that would become the dam. He did finish it, it did hold water, and he stocked it with catfish.

I share this silly story as an example of how to experience flow in conquest. Putting in the time day after day was Dad's way of wrestling well. As I recalled this story during my time of personal healing, six words came to mind that helped free me from the bondage of how poorly I used to wrestle with life. They have set me on the path of healthy conquest. The things I strive for and accomplish now no longer add to my burdens and pain; instead, they fuel the peace, joy, and love I have come to know so intimately. The words are *clarity, tenacity, patience, wisdom, motivation,* and *passion.*

Be Sure You Are Charging Up the Right Hill

The quote at the beginning of this chapter is one of the best quotes from my favorite movie. It points to the importance of responding to the present moment. I have wasted a lot of time, fighting the wrong battles, charging up the wrong hills and leaving myself very little to show for it except the bumps and bruises of my failed conquests. Wrestling is a part of who we are. No; not the kind where you dress in the funny-looking, tight suit and beat up your opponent, but the kind where you battle through difficulties, solve problems, and overcome struggles—you know, life. I told you my dad taught me a lot about how to wrestle well. What I didn't say is that it took me a long time and a lot of failure for that learning to stick.

I used to be very good at wrestling with all the wrong things. But, if you needed someone in your corner to deal with a big difficulty or struggle, I was your partner. I would go to the mat for you. I wouldn't quit until we made things better. Personal struggles, community needs, disasters . . . you name it, and I was there. I would lead the charge up the hill, dig in deep, and not stop wrestling until we had conquered. Wait . . . people and communities in need and disasters don't sound like bad or wrong things to wrestle for, right? In and of themselves, no; of course, they don't. But my wrestling came at a great cost to me. Too many times, I was wrestling in those arenas for the wrong reasons, at the wrong times, and even to my own detriment. But good still came from my efforts. Like I have said before, God can speak through rocks and jackasses, so He also used me in many great ways. I am thankful and blessed for that.

So, what was the cost? I spent years giving myself to help others while never feeling worthy of asking anyone to help me. I jumped into whatever project or opportunity came my direction if it helped people. And as I've had occasion to point out already, my helping was also a kind of avoiding. If I was serving people, I did not have to think as much about how broken I was. When I was contending with the needs of others, I could not hear the incessant screams of the internal monsters reminding me how terribly worthless I was. So, you see, what I wrestled for—helping those in need—was not inherently bad. But doing so from such an empty tank of self-worth took its toll. I could never sit still. I was always involved in starting another project. I could only avoid dealing with my own pain and brokenness if I was helping others with theirs. It is like I became addicted to serving the needs of others so I could ignore my own. I was envious, almost jealous of my dad's ability to be so tenacious in completing things he set his mind to. One day, I asked him what the secret was to his tenacity and never-give-up attitude. Again, with that simple, country-boy philosophy, he looked at me and said, "If you know you are charging up the right hill, nothing will stop you. It takes doing your homework to have the clarity to know that where you are and what you are doing means something to you." He had gotten clarity before starting work on that pond. He studied the soil and the way the water flowed when it rained. He knew having his own pond would bring him joy, no matter how silly people thought he was for the way he built it. So, that was his hill at that moment. It was important to him, and he was all there; he had gotten clarity that he was making the best choices, ones that would bring him a return of many hours of joy fishing on his own pond.

That is where I always got hung up. I was never all there. I found clarity that there were needs on the next hill, but I intentionally blinded myself to the truth: I was in no shape, mentally or emotionally, to be charging up any hill unless it was going to attack my own inner monsters. I don't regret the hills I charged and the things I wrestled with in helping others; I cannot allow regret to poison the joy and peace I now have in life. But I know I let a lot of people down by not being all there, by always bouncing from one thing to another, trying to save the world.

Honestly, I know I let myself down, too. That I lacked clarity was all on me. That it took me so long to get the help I gave others was also all on me. If I had taken a better look at things before going all in, I might have noticed my brokenness; I might have addressed my pain sooner. Instead, I got good at seeing the world around me from my smile forward. Everything in front of my smile meant something, but there was nothing good behind the smile. Dad said, "Have the clarity to know that what you are doing and where you are both have meaning." Like a lot of my life before healing, my outside world and my inside world were not in sync. It is hard to be fully present when there is chaos in your heart and mind. That is the opposite of clarity. I did not have tenacity then, because seeing things through was not my primary motivation—quieting the monsters was. I am so thankful I finally broke free from that lie and bondage.

You were wired to wrestle, to achieve, to experience conquest in your life, whether it be for you, your family, your career, or the good of others. But be sure you are charging up the right hill. It might look good at first glance but be sure you can be all there before advancing. It is great to be there for others but be there for yourself as much. Be sure you have been tenacious in contending for your own needs. Being all there means your body, soul, mind, and heart are all in sync. If you have clarity, all your systems will agree with one another. If not, then you know the first hill you need to charge is inside you. Get right with yourself; then you will have what it takes to wrestle with the challenges of life. I wish I had known that a long time ago. If you feel clarity in your self-assessment, believe it is your hill, and are fully there, charge it. Charge those hills and never give up.

The Art of the Question

We seem to have become a culture of people afraid to ask questions. Many see it as a sign of weakness. Others struggle with the belief that people will think they are dumb. Okay, men, you know we are at the top of that list. We like to have all the answers, and if we get lost on a trip, by gosh, the last thing we want to do is stop and ask a stranger for help with directions.

But I have learned that a well-asked question, like vulnerability, is one of the strongest and most courageous things you can do. While I have reaped many benefits from surrounding myself with others whom I could trust with my questions, I learned that one of the most powerful uses of asking good questions is with myself. I teach every client this self-check process to use before making big decisions.

Our brains are like a computer. Introduce a problem or any unknown and the thinking part kicks in and endeavors to find a solution. Leveraging this and building it into a habit will not only help you have more wisdom in your decision-making, but it will help develop patience as well. Let's unpack this simple and effective process. Just remember the letters, QEDLG (question, explore, discover, learn, grow).

Question. Never be afraid to ask questions of others or yourself. Do not give in to that (mostly male) problem of thinking others will think you are dumb or lazy for asking a question. Asking yourself a question before making a challenging decision shifts your brain from the act without thinking mode to problem-solving mode. Embrace that. Do the courageous and vulnerable thing by making it a habit to ask better questions.

Explore. Once you have sparked the brain to consider possibilities in response to your question, now it is time to wrestle with the options. Think through where each answer or potential path may take you. It is okay to ask questions of your questions. The more you dig, the more you find, and the more solid and educated your choice will be.

Discover. Be intentional with what you observe on the path of exploration. One question may awaken discovery that will be pertinent in several other areas of your life. You never know when something of little value in your current focus of exploration may help you in later endeavors.

Learn. Whether you commit to memory, work on developing a habit, or journal your process, be sure you are fully present with it. This is a building process. Questions lead to exploration, which leads to discovery, which leads to learning. Remember, the only bad question is the one you do not ask. Asking yourself better questions and following this process will help you to be more present, more at peace, and more certain of the choices you make.

Grow. There will be a certain amount of natural growth with this process but being intentional and present with it is imperative. For everything you learn, ask yourself these questions:

- Is this the best possible outcome to deal with the problem or challenge before me?

- Does it move me closer to the pursuit of my passion in life, or at least, bring peace and joy in the moment?

- Does it help me with my goal of becoming a better version of myself than I was yesterday?

The opposite of this process usually breeds chaos. The shoot-from-the-hip approach I took most of my life left me questioning my motives, lacking in clarity, and feeling more confusion than peace and calm. The crazy thing is, I asked just as many questions of myself, but they lacked intention and forethought. I was always second-guessing myself. Many anxiety sufferers and those holding on to hacked narratives of past trauma behave this same way. But that is no excuse. You can wrestle through life without focus or clarity, never experiencing growth, or you can choose to take captive the narrative process in your mind and do better. You are stronger than you think. Wisdom comes from doing the hard work and patience comes from practice.

Warrior or Worrier

Let me start by saying I am not bashing anyone with what I am about to share. I have wrestled with life from the point of view of both mindsets. In all honesty, I have spent more of my years as a worrier than as a warrior, so I believe I have some insight into both. I can spot the armor-clad worrier from miles away. Open almost any social media platform and there they are. But do not sell the worrier mindset short. They can be bullish in their approaches when wrestling with the challenges of life, as well as with you. But their greatest fault is that they usually operate from a base of fear. They are zealous in their opinions and easily take offense if you disagree with them. They feel like an attack on their opinions is an attack on them. They are not all bad. Many times, their motives are to help others and to do good. But worry usually overtakes their ability to be fully present and objective.

This was me for more years than I would like to admit. I thought if you did not like what I said, then you did not like me. I needed my opinions and ideas to be validated so I could feel validated as a person. This is the way a person operates when they lack self-confidence and value in themselves. They look to the world to give them what they should naturally have within themselves. When things do not go the way of the worrier, they often respond with anger or anxiety, depending on how they process chaos. I could never be angry at anyone except myself, so I was always the anxious one left to fight the chaos of my internal narrative with a smile on my face.

The warrior mindset operates from a base of self-confidence instead of fear. They are at peace with whom they are and do not require outside influences or people to validate their belief or their self-value. The warrior mindset seeks understanding rather than just agreement. They are motivated to make decisions that preserve peace and joy and move them forward in becoming better versions of themselves.

As a worrier, busyness was my measure of success. The more I was involved in, the more hills I was charging up, the more validated and worthy I was. As a warrior, I only wrestle with things that I can control or influence. If it is outside that realm, whether it be for me or others, then it is not my hill to charge. This was a saving grace for me during my quest for freedom. It helped me to quiet my mind and listen better to the broken internal narratives that were driving my life. It brought me the clarity that my dad was always trying to teach me.

So, how do you know what to wrestle with, what hills and challenges to engage? You should wrestle with

- things you can control or influence,
- things that bring healing, peace, and calm,
- things that move you closer to your passion in life, and
- things that help you become a better version of yourself.

You should avoid wrestling with,

- things outside your control,

- things that really do not matter in the grand scheme (i.e., most social media arguments),

- things where you are only trying to prove yourself right over others, and

- things that hinder your peace, joy, or forward movement.

Life is short and you only have so much physical, mental, and emotional energy at any given time. Make sure you have clarity and focus on choosing what to wrestle with and what hills to charge. And if you have mental health issues as I did, no hill is worth charging more than taking care of yourself first. You deserve to be whole and present. Your own peace and joy are the conquests that will make the others all the sweeter. Here is the thought that I planted deep in my mind when I was working to find freedom and healing. It was a paradigm shift for me in deciding what in my life was worth wrestling with and what needed to be let go. Like my dad taught me, be sure the hill you are charging is one you are meant to be on. Does it better who you are? Is it a hill you would be willing to die on?

There was a time I thought they all were. I learned those who are the most broken are the ones who feel the hardest. They charge all the hills and want to help all the people because they do not want anyone to hurt as they do inside. That was me, but that was not my best. I had to fix myself. And doing that brought me all the things I fought for so many years to attain; joy, peace, love, and most of all, belief in and acceptance of myself.

Embracing Light

- An unbroken shovel digs a hole better than a broken one. The same goes for you. You deserve to embrace life whole and full of joy and peace. Until you have that freedom, there is nothing more important to wrestle with.

- Avoidance of your own needs will bring chaos where you need clarity. It bears repeating: Self-care is not selfish.

- The only dumb question is the one not asked. Embrace the process of QEDLG.

- Be brave enough to ask yourself deep, probing questions, and be vulnerable enough to never accept easy, surface-level answers.

- Busyness and being involved in everything that crosses your path do not equal success. Conversely, it can slowly tear down your world.

- Do not live from the mindset of the worrier. Fear will get you nothing you deserve and everything you don't need. When you decide to face your fears, they immediately begin to lose power.

- Wrestle with those things you can control and influence. Let everything else go. Make sure the conquests you strive for help you be a better version of yourself.

- When charging the hills in life, ask yourself, "Is this a hill I am willing to die on?"

13

INTIMACY

Embracing Flow in Compassion

Seek first to understand, then to be understood.
—Stephen Covey

My understanding of intimacy was broken for me as a child, and I carried that brokenness with me for too many years. I started sixth grade at a new school, and I was quite uncomfortable that I did not know anyone. For reasons I still cannot understand, I accepted a dare that got me sent to the principal's office. I said something about a girl being pretty and some boys said, "Then why don't you go kiss her?" So, I did. I walked right up to her, said hello, and kissed her on the mouth. She ran off screaming and told on me. This led to a brief lecture about intimacy, sex, and boundaries, in which my teacher defined intimacy for me as, "When two people are in love."

She lost me there. I couldn't hear anything else she was saying. It sounded like she was equating intimacy with sex, and sex scared me. Sex was about manipulation and doing what you were told, and it was painful. There is nothing about being sexually abused that feels intimate.

Boundaries can be difficult enough without sexual abuse. I would spend years misunderstanding true intimacy. Children who are sexually abused get exposed to things years before they own the mental capacity to understand them. A big part of my bondage was not understanding the authentic nature of intimacy, especially when it came to loving myself. During my healing journey, I poured my efforts deeply into understanding intimacy and through that, learned to love myself and others from my soul and not just my feelings. Yes, sex is a part of intimacy, but it is the icing on the cake. Learning the beautiful process of baking the cake (i.e., embracing the fullness of intimacy) is the sweetest part of love and compassion.

Okay, so intimacy is not just about sex. Then what is it about? It is about experiencing an extreme emotional connection or closeness with someone. It is entering someone's bubble or space, with permission and invitation. If life were a dance, intimacy would be a slow dance. There are many types or levels of it to be experienced, with only one of them entailing touch. We can be emotionally intimate with someone through simple and vulnerable conversation. Mental intimacy would be when we find and embrace common ground or common interests together. Connecting, together, to God or to something bigger than both of us would be intimacy at the spiritual level. Even physical intimacy has many levels besides just sex. It may be more correct to say physical intimacy is the icing on the cake, and sex is the cherry on top.

So how do we experience flow in intimacy, and where does compassion fit in? Remember, flow is having clarity or focus, being fully present, and experiencing joy in the moment. What my dad always said is a beautiful example of having flow in life: "Wherever you are and whoever you are with, treat that as the most important person/moment in your life." When I think about intimacy, I recall words like trust, acceptance, honesty, vulnerability, safety, compassion, and communication. All of those are important in having an intimate connection with someone, but compassion, to me, is the engine that drives all the others. To show compassion is to be aware or conscious of someone else's needs, pain, or distress and having an intense, soul-level desire to fulfill or alleviate that need. Doesn't the world need more compassion? Don't we all need more of it?

No Labels Required

Labels. Adjectives. *Them* and *those people*. Some words create worlds where human beings are lined up in a pecking order. I am so tired of our culture feeling the need to assign unnecessary descriptions to people, to keep them corded off in convenient herds of similar-looking and similar-thinking individuals. Why can't we all just be fellow human beings? I know some of you may think I am being fussy, and I am aware that some people are okay with wearing certain labels. But far too much of the labeling is due to hate and fear, and it damages our ability to show compassion, experience intimacy, and know authentic love. I shared this with someone in a coffee shop once, and their response was, "I am just fine showing compassion and love to my own kind of people." That broke my heart. All I could do was share my differing opinion and show that person love and, yes, compassion. After twenty years of working with others and through my own journey from self-hate to being able to show compassion to myself, I have learned that fear is the main cause of our lack of experiencing it or showing it to others.

Nowhere in our culture is this more evident than on social media. So many people keep walls up to separate themselves from people that think, act, or look different from them. They hide behind man-made comfort zones, shout their disapproval, and often hate at anything or anyone who stands contrary to what they believe or think. This kind of behavior damages our hearts and souls. It hinders our capacity to be fully present and show compassion, even to those we accept and welcome into our space. While our hacked narratives can wire us to experience fear and hate, we are all God-wired to experience fullness in life through love and compassion. We were not wired for fear or hate.

I don't know if it results from the early sexual abuse or if it is just part of my nature, but I have never been able to hate or judge others. As I said before, the only person I have ever hated is myself. I never even hated either of my abusers. I never wanted to humiliate them or throw them under a bus. Why? Because it would have done nothing good for me. I found my freedom from that experience in the same place where my bondage was—inside me. If I had had the opportunity to talk to either of them, I would have forgiven them. I would have asked them only one question and given only one response. I would have asked them what hurt they experienced that enabled them to cause someone else such pain? And I would have told them I hoped when they found that answer, they would find freedom and healing for themselves. I know the power of that question and comment intimately. It is what I asked of myself when I awakened to the fullness of the bondage I was living in and the pain I had caused others at times in my life. The answers humbled and hurt me, but they also, ultimately, brought me the into the light of freedom and healing.

We do not need to put labels on people. We do not need to say *liberal* or *conservative* him, or *black*, *brown*, or *white* her. And we do not constantly need to heap blame and hate for the problems of the world on "them" or "those people." May we find the courage to just be fellow passengers on this tiny rock we call Earth? We all need compassion. We all hunger for intimacy. Maybe a lot of the problems of the world would be solved if we stopped staying so separated behind our walls of fear and just embraced one another with the compassion and intimacy we desire for ourselves. Maybe I am too hopeful.

Maybe I wish for something out of reach. But working for that is where I will hang my hat. It is a hill worth dying on.

All We Need Is

I can hear all you Beatles fans now. All we need is *love*, right? That is true, but I want to point out three things that we are all wired to desire. Living without one or all of them can have catastrophic results in our relationships, our views of life, and our own minds. Being heard, valued, and understood is integral to our experience of intimacy. I believe we need all three of these to experience compassion for others. Not one person would disagree with how valuable these three things are to them. So why do we see so many people in our culture struggle to be able to give or receive these beautiful gifts?

It was a Wednesday morning. Things were drastically different. Getting up and getting breakfast ready for the family was surreal. We were more intentional in every move we made. We hugged longer and did not want to be apart from each other. That night, we attended a prayer meeting at church. The environment there was also surreal. Family, friends, and strangers treated one another equally. There were no labels, no separation. We showed and experienced compassion without judgment. The moments were filled with a level of spiritual, emotional, and mental intimacy that was palpable. We all showed our hunger for feeling heard, valued, and understood by one another without fear or trepidation. It was September 12, 2001. Disasters change our mental economy. There is no place for hate. There is no time to fear or overthink things. I don't think September 12 brought out something fake or manufactured; I think that is our true character as humans. I think all the other "normal" days of life cloud our judgments, and bring out the fear, hate, and separation. Wouldn't it be amazing if we trusted our souls to show compassion and intimacy the way we were created to?

I failed to feel heard, valued, and understood for much of my life. It would be easy to blame it on my past or to levy the fault on those around me, but that suggests I was powerless. In fact, I had the power to change my thinking, and to change my beliefs, I just didn't know it yet. In school, I always wore a smile; I loved my friends, and I had a lot of great experiences. But, during much of it, I was an empty shell. I had the same experience while attending church as a kid. I felt distant in almost every environment. I hungered to belong, but at the same time, I felt like a fraud who did not deserve to be heard, valued, or understood. When I awakened to my internal narrative, I could hear the monsters of my past trauma telling me to fear intimacy. My mind equated getting close to others with the "closeness" I experienced in my abuse. I failed to connect with others for so long, especially as a child and young adult. I wore masks to try to be what I thought others wanted me to be, and sex was the center of every close female relationship. All the while, I hated who I believed I was inside. Everywhere I went, there it was, the hate.

I struggled to feel and get from others what I could not give myself. But that's not intimacy; it's more like vampirism or parasitism. If we want to experience being heard, valued, and understood, then we must work to hear ourselves, value ourselves, and understand who we truly are.

What Are You Really Looking For?

Our culture places a heavy emphasis on caring for the body, our outside self, but many of us are afraid to give that same level of attention to caring for our mental and emotional well-being. There is a stigma associated with needing help with mental health struggles. So, we get our manicures, pedicures, massages, and facials, but often ignore the needs of our heart, mind, and soul. We are wired for such needs, so it should come as no surprise that we have pain and dysfunction when ignoring them. If we eat poorly and don't take care of our bodies, we aren't surprised by weight gain and medical problems. If we relate to ourselves or others poorly, we shouldn't be surprised that we have unhealthy relationships.

Why do we fear intimacy? Why do we mistrust compassion? Clients often tell me, "Every time I open myself up to someone, I get hurt." I can't deny that may be true sometimes, but I think more harm is done by closing ourselves up in the prison of our comfort zones. More times than not, the problem lies with our perspective as much or more than with another person. I know that was true for me, as it is for many who struggle with past trauma and hacked beliefs about themselves.

I knew I hated myself for a long time. But I still wondered why that brought struggles in so many other areas of my life. Then, during a time of prayer and asking deep questions of myself, I found what I think were the reasons I struggled. Although I am sure not all my readers will share my viewpoint, my belief in God and my relationship with Jesus was paramount in my journey to freedom and healing. So, it makes sense that one of the core lessons I needed to learn, to heal from my past, concerned my relationship with God. If things like compassion, intimacy, belonging, and feeling valued are the engine that drives me, then I learned the gasoline was my understanding and acceptance of God's redemption, renewal, and restoration of my soul.

I had the first part—the understanding—down ever since I gave Him my life in 1988, but the acceptance was something that had gone dormant through my years of bondage and self-hate. That was something everyone else deserved, but I had to work to attain it one day. During my wrestling with God on the side of that mountain in Tennessee, He showed me how I had left those things on the table. They were mine for the taking. His grace and mercy paved the way for me to own those things in my daily life. But I was not worthy, or so I believed. Here is what he revealed to me.

In the book of Genesis, Adam and Eve had disobeyed God. He told them they would have consequences for their choices, but then He turned right around and redeemed them. He clothed their naked bodies and provided a way for them (Gn. 3:1–21). It is as if God were saying to me, "Did they do anything to deserve my redemption? No; it was because I loved them, the same as I do you. You have struggled through your consequences. You have beaten yourself up. You hurt yourself and others. Now, learn from what happened. I love you and you are redeemed."

In the twenty-second Psalm, David catalogs his suffering, lashing out at God and asking Him why He had forsaken him (Ps. 22:1–2). I did the same thing on that mountainside. But as the conversation goes in David's heart, he comes to the realization that God had done none of those things to him. His circumstances were all due to his choices and the choices of others. What he realized was that God was always there, offering his love through the renewal of his heart. This was the same for me. When I yelled at and even cursed God, he showed me the same thing. This is what I heard Him say in my heart: *You suffered greatly as a child because of others' choices. You also suffered greatly because of your own choices and mistakes. But I was always there, one step away. You never experienced renewal because you never asked. Now that you have asked, what have I done? Everything.* He renewed me fully in the moment of brokenness and acknowledging my need for Him.

Peter had stated that he would never leave or deny Jesus (Matt. 26:33). But what did he do when the going got tough? On the night Jesus was arrested, Peter denied knowing him three times and ran into hiding with his fear and shame (Matt. 26:66–74). What did Jesus do? He did not punish him or rebuke him. He knew Peter had already experienced the pain and consequences of his choices. In the twenty-first chapter of the book of John, Jesus met Peter at the point of his need. Over a breakfast of fish and an illustration of feeding sheep,

Jesus restored Peter (John 21:15–17). He loved him in the exact way he needed to reconnect to his true self.

I felt too ashamed to accept those things from God for a long time. I believed in Him and gave my whole life to Him (well, almost all of it), but I never fully trusted Him with my deepest and darkest pain. I would not be freed, healed, or writing this book without understanding, accepting, and experiencing the fullness of God's redemption, renewal, and restoration of my life. It is what allowed me to reconnect to my soul, to know myself truly. If you do not already know this truth in your soul, I pray you will find your connection to it soon.

What Did Jesus Do?

I do not, personally, know a better image of what intimacy with our fellow humans looks like than in the life of Jesus. Now I am not talking about religion and fitting any pre-conceived notions of other humans; I am talking about Jesus' example of what a real relationship with others should look like. He showed empathy and compassion to all who crossed His path. He spoke the truth, but he spoke it wrapped heavily in love.

How did Jesus love those different from Him? He sat in the courtyard or by the well and intimately connected to them in conversation. He went to their homes for dinner, and He attended their parties. How did He love those that opposed Him? He spoke truth to them, in love. He shared with them in nighttime conversation. He offered them compassion. He showed by His life that offering redemption, renewal, and restoration to *all* was a hill worth dying on—literally. He never overlooked or condoned their faults and mistakes, but He never beat them over the head with them, either (gleaned from the combined Scriptures of Matthew, Mark, Luke, and John). God does not leave us at the point of our greatest failures or mistakes, so neither should we leave ourselves or others there.

If God loves us like this, regardless of whether we struggle to accept it, how much more should we love ourselves and others? Do not fear intimacy. You were wired for that connection. Your soul is never more alive than when you offer yourself and others the opportunity to be heard, valued, and understood. And then, the icing on the cake of intimacy is the ability to show it to all around us through acts of compassion. Now that is some flow where I find great joy in experiencing.

Go to Where?

One extra tidbit as we close this chapter. Before I share this, let me say I enjoy remembering things by using acrostics. I used them in grad school, and I use them often with clients. I have learned that the funnier or odder they are, the easier they are to commit to memory. So, here is one I truly love that helps me remember I deserve intimacy and compassion for myself every day. Also, it helps me focus on sharing that intimacy and compassion with others I cross paths with as well.

We should strive to go to HELL with others every day. See, I told you it was odd, especially coming from the guy who just wrote a whole section about God. But every client I have ever shared this with acknowledges that it is impossible to forget and invaluable in reminding them to show themselves and others love and compassion. What's in HELL (*h*ug, *e*ye contact, *l*augh, *l*isten)? Let's have a look:

Hug – Be sure to give and get at least one hug a day. Science has even shown that a good, long, healthy hug reduces cortisol, the stress hormone, and increases serotonin, the mood-stabilizing hormone.

Eye contact – Put down the phone, reign in your focus, and be present with others. Look them in the eye when you engage them. It makes people feel heard, valued, and understood.

Laugh – Laughter truly is the best medicine. I meet clients often who say they cannot remember the last time they had a good laugh. Let yourself go some during the day. Stop being so serious, worried, or anxious and have a good, long belly laugh. It is good for whatever ails you.

Listen – Do not just hear people or situations around you; listen. Truly listen without judgment and with empathy and compassion. We miss so many opportunities for intimate connections with others because we listen so poorly. Again, put down the phone and look at all the life right in front of you.

We need to stop being afraid to connect to others. If we fear anything, it should be the loss of the ability to connect. And be sure you are the first one you connect with. I missed out on feeling a lot of compassion from those around me, not because it wasn't offered, but because I had none for myself. Be brave. Love yourself. Forgive yourself. Life is too short to stay stuck or in bondage.

Embracing Light

- Authentic compassion requires being in flow. We must have clarity and focus, be fully present in the moment, and experience joy to engage one another at the point of need. We all hunger for it. We all need it.

- Accept people for who they are—people. There is no need for labels to keep you safely separated from others. That does not mean you have to accept or agree with all they believe or stand for. It means you acknowledge you are both flawed, imperfect, and in need of being heard, valued, and understood.

- Hate and fear will always block your ability to truly know intimacy or compassion for others and yourself. If you think you lack intimacy in life, look at what fear might keep you from being free to experience it.

- Redemption, renewal, and restoration bring freedom to our souls. You deserve it, regardless of whether you feel that way. If you do not feel that presence in your life, connect with someone who will help you on that journey.

- This kind of HELL is not a bad place. Be sure all your days include a good hug, eye contact with another human, a good belly laugh, and the experience of truly being present and listening to those engaging you.

14

SYMPHONY

Embracing Flow in Community

*There is no greater agony than bearing
an untold story inside you.*
—Maya Angelou

What is community? It can be a group of people joined together by physical proximity or by a particular commonality. My wife and I are a part of a community where we live, made up of people from very different backgrounds and beliefs, but we are drawn together by our shared interest in taking care of our little corner of the world. We are also a part of a small community of Jesus followers, but that is where the commonality between us goes in different directions. We are made up of sports enthusiasts, self-professed nerds, families with children, and older families whose children are all grown.

Both groups are drawn and held together through our shared desire to watch out for one another. We practice compassion as we meet one another at the point of our needs. We share intimacy together in shared projects, shared meals, and shared moments of conversation, outside under the stars or around the pool. Everyone realizes we are imperfect individuals who have flaws and have made mistakes, but we strive to ensure that love leads the way in how we treat one another. We embrace the truth that together we are stronger. All involved clearly realize that doing life together in a community helps us to get out of our heads and see life more objectively and realistically. No one is an island, and we often invite extra sets of eyes and ears into our life situations or struggles. An authentic community is an enlarged safe space of the family where we promise no judgment of one another and strive to help each member be a better version of ourselves.

My life is a living testament that just being surrounded by a big group of people does not constitute a community. Throughout my life, I have been invited into many kinds of groups. I do not remember a time that I was alienated or rejected by any community group, but there were many times where I alienated and rejected myself. My lack of self-worth, the myriad of limiting beliefs, and the lies I held onto hindered my ability to stay a part of the communities. I was usually very excited to join a new group of people, enjoyed the honeymoon period, and then slowly faded behind the curtain until I found a new group. I know I missed out on many rich friendships from being this way, for leaving the group for fear they would discover my worthlessness. While I was motivated to add to the community, those things most important to its existence—to share knowledge, help one another problem solve, share love, compassion, and intimacy—I always felt I personally deserved none of this.

I learned an important lesson in my quest for freedom and healing. To thrive in a community, you must first be adept at thriving within yourself. I was terrible at that for many years. Rather than allow my internal chaos to poison the group, it seemed better to me to put up a facade and be all things to all people for as long as I could and then exit when I lost the ability to do that. I got good at smiling on the outside and hurting on the inside. It was great to finally shine a light on that darkness and find freedom.

Life is hard and we never know the story someone is living. We should all treat one another like we do on the day after a huge disaster, as we talked about in the last chapter. I am not alone in the way I fought internal wars while looking peaceful and joyful on the outside. There are millions of us, and like all of us, those struggling, hurting, and imperfect humans need community. Our lives depend on it. It is crazy to see many who struggle with mental health issues avoid the light of community when it is the exact thing needed to help them get free. Are you a part of one or more communities? If so, I applaud you. Embrace compassion. Seek out the good in others. Help them become better versions of themselves. I bet the favor will be returned. If you are not a part of a community in any way, I recommend changing that quickly. Life is a symphony, and we are all called to be a part of the orchestra that makes beautiful music together.

He Plays His Part Well

It was early on a hot summer day in August where I live in Tyler, Texas. I was walking the streets of one neighborhood that had a lot of homes in disrepair. I was part of a non-profit group that painted homes and did small repairs for low-income families and the elderly. I was scouting for homes that needed painting for a group of one hundred college-student volunteers that were coming to help. One street over from me, I heard a loud garbage truck making the rounds, and in between its starting and stopping, I heard the most beautiful whistling. I had to go see who or what it was. It turned out to be one of the city sanitation workers with the truck. He was walking down the street, emptying people's trash into the truck, and whistling like nobody's business. I have never met a stranger and will engage anyone who crosses my path. We said hello to one another, and I had to ask him.

"What's got you so happy this morning?"

"I am upright and breathing, the sun is shining, and I have my health, so I am full of joy." He told me he had been married for forty years, lived in a simple but paid-off house, and was blessed as a trash man to encounter sweet elderly folks and shut-ins along his route.

"This is my community," he proudly stated. "I love these people, and I may be the only face they encounter today, so I want to share some of my joy. That's why I whistle as I work." His response has been etched on my heart for more than twelve years, and I still refer to him as one of the happiest men in Tyler, Texas.

Community, for this kind man, had nothing to do with what a lot of people look to be a part of. He had little money, was not famous, and lived in one of the poorest parts of the city. But he had the core of what community is all about. He was a part of life with these people, the symphony, and he played his part well. He found belonging in shared compassion, acceptance, and authentic love for others. I would say he was one of the richest men I have ever met.

On a more comical note, I saw the most hilarious video recently of a man playing the triangle in an orchestra. You know that little triangle-shaped piece of shiny metal that you hit with another straight, shiny piece of metal. Usually, that instrument is one that you can barely hear among the strings, brass, and percussion sections of the orchestra. But this triangle player had been given a solo in the performance. He didn't just stand up and play his part, but he came to the front and proceeded to moonwalk across the stage as he struck his triangle with joy. It was a hilarious sight, but it drove home a point about community. Like the trash man, he owned his role well. He played his part as if everyone else in the community (i.e., orchestra) was relying on his success. He was not caught up in comparing himself to the violin section or the loud bass

WE ARE ALL FIREFLIES

drum; he did what he was gifted and able to do to ensure the success of the rest of the group.

The trash collector and the triangle player—what a beautiful picture of community they were. They both had joy and peace for the role they played for others. They experienced the three key aspects of flow in the community: belonging, love, and purpose.

May you play your part well in whatever community you find yourself a part of. Thankfully, I finally found the freedom to feel worthy to be a true part of a community. The blessings I have experienced in groups in the past were only the tip of the iceberg once I finally embraced a belief in myself and accepted and loved myself.

Our Longing for Belonging

No matter who you are, we all hunger for acceptance. It starts in us when we are infants. Not only do we require the help of our parents or caretakers, but our soul longs for it. You do not have to look any further than babies to understand the power of belonging or the power of missing out on it. Infants who are neglected and miss out on human touch for the first couple of years of their lives often struggle with mental and emotional health issues for many years, even into adulthood. The lack of true belonging is at catastrophic levels in many areas of our culture. If the world of social media hadn't already done enough to isolate many people behind their screens, then 2020 came along and ripped many communities apart. I think it will be months and years to come before we see the effects on our mental health from the isolation that so many people live in today.

My longing for belonging used to be like a never-ending hunger. I had no problem drawing close to others, and I was comfortable in crowds of people, but the inside of my head was like a fireworks factory going up in flames. Like everyone else,

169

I had the need for acceptance and the security of belonging to a community, but I was constantly asking myself if I was being enough for everyone. Was I making this person happy enough? Did I help this person enough with their problems? Why can't I feel as accepted as they are? It was incessant. I could never fully know belonging because I felt I was never worthy to belong with anyone. I know I have said it here in several ways before, but I want to be sure you sense the gravity of the struggle experienced by those in bondage to a trauma narrative. Maybe it's you. Or maybe it is a loved one or friend, and you have struggled with wanting to say to them, "Just stop thinking about those things and get over it." Even if you feel like it, please do not say that. It is hard to understand, but the person entrenched in the pain of a hacked internal narrative must awaken to the need for help before they can change. There must be an impetus, like a sudden wave of self-awareness or a train wreck. Unfortunately, too many of us require a train wreck.

If we would embrace who we truly are—fearfully and wonderfully made, imperfect, and with flaws—we could better embrace community with others. But many of us struggle with comparison and thinking we must compete with others to be better than they. My big struggle was thinking I had to be what everyone expected me to be. That added to my internal chaos. A lot of people also miss out on having a sense of belonging within a community because they think it must be made up of people exactly like them. If that describes you, I want to say you are missing out on some potentially amazing experiences.

We have some friends who are very close to one another and experience a deep sense of community in their small group of friends. These two women met over a difference they had with one another. It started as a random conversation in a coffee shop, but when the chat turned political, they learned they were on opposite sides of the aisle. One joked with the other.

"Well, I guess we can't be friends now." After they both pondered that statement, the other lady responded. "Or we can just talk about everything else except politics." They have now enjoyed a friendship of many years that has birthed and grown into a larger community of people doing life together.

You do not have to experience belonging with cookie-cutter versions of yourself. What fun is that? Besides, you get what you look for the hardest in people. If you look for differences or flaws in them, you are going to find them, in others as well as yourself. But if you look for the good, often, you are going to find it. My wife and I enjoy a community of friends on different sides of the political aisle, of different colors and persuasions. Some have much more money than we do, and some do not have as much. We work hard to build true community and a sense of belonging. Why? Because it makes life richer. We learn from one another. We have each other's backs, and we are motivated to help one another become better versions of ourselves.

Trust the Good Stuff

Songs and poems have been written about the good stuff. Some of my favorite movies are about searching for it, losing it, and finding your forever connection to it. What am I talking about? Love. All we need is love. Love is all around us. Love makes the world go round. Okay, I am done being hokey. But it is true. Real love, the authentic form of it, really is all those things and more. But our world suffers greatly from impostor love. What is that you say? Imposter love is self-seeking, conditional, and controlling. That is the exact opposite of love, but it is what I see a lot of people giving and receiving. Like many things, I think the main motivator for that type of behavior is fear.

Too many of us fear really opening ourselves up to authentic love, whether it be the intimate love of a couple, or the kind of love felt within a community of friends. Our culture has conditioned us to put up a front to protect ourselves from being real and vulnerable with those around us. Can authentic love sometimes be painful? Yes. But you know what can be even more painful and destructive? Thinking that imposter love is ever going to fulfill you. Even worse is the pain felt by those that have just given up on love completely. Our culture has it backward. Love is about being selfless, not selfish. It is about showing compassion for the good of others, not just seeking our own good. And it is not the "you complete me" bull that Hollywood tries to serve us. Here is a newsflash if you did not already know it: I do not care if you fall in love with the most perfect human on the planet; they do not have the power to complete you. That is *your* work. I believed that lie for far too long. It caused me great pain and almost destroyed all I hold dear in life. It put undue pressure on my wife to try to measure up to a level she was not created for. I needed someone to complete me because I could not find completion myself. God could not even complete me for a long time, not because He was not powerful enough, but because I did not believe I was worthy to ask for it.

Regardless of whether you believe in God, I have never found a more perfect picture of what authentic love should look like than in the Bible in the thirteenth chapter of First Corinthians. I am not going to quote it all here, but I implore you to go read it, even if you have heard it a hundred times before. It is beautiful. Love is patient and kind and does not seek to serve self. Love looks out for the good of others. Love never quits or gives up. Love never loses its grip on faith and hope (1Cor. 13:1–7). Wow, that is being in flow! That kind of love could change the world. It could change your world. A community with that kind of love would be a force to be reckoned with. It is yours for the asking. It only takes releasing all your preconceived notions about love, trusting your heart to endure the hurt you may encounter, and never, ever giving up. I pray you know that love in more and more ways, with more and more people, all the days of your life. I would never have found freedom without it. My soul would never have healed without it. And you would not be reading this book right now without the power of that light-filled, beautiful, unconditional love.

The Power of Purpose

Purpose is the reason we do things or our planned intention. Let me start by bursting the bubble on things I have heard some people say. Your purpose in life is not to keep the yard mowed, the family fed, and to faithfully punch the clock at work five days a week. Those are tasks or responsibilities. Now, hopefully, you gain joy or a sense of satisfaction from keeping your family fed. And punching that clock at work may provide the funds to pursue your purpose or passion in life. But your purpose in life is something that sets your soul on fire. That thing that stirs a passion inside you, that you cannot stop thinking about. Your purpose, once embraced, is what becomes the stuff of legacy for your loved ones after you are gone.

A community of people living out their purpose in life stirs compassion for one another among its members. One person, on fire with purpose and passion, can ignite the souls of all those around them to discover their own God-given purpose in life. Some people are blessed to get paid to live out their purpose. I have a family member who is a surgeon. It is his job and the way he feeds his family. But it is also the thing that lights up his life, the thing that gets him out of bed in the morning. No matter whether you get paid to pursue your life's purpose or not, we are wired for it. Having a purpose in life reduces stress, makes life less chaotic, helps us to be more others-centered, and helps to fuel hope in our hearts. A person lacking in purpose often struggles with deep-seated mental health issues.

What is your purpose in life? If you know it, are you embracing it and living it out? If you do not feel you know your life's purpose or what brings you passion, now is the time to discover that. You deserve it, and the community of people you do life with will benefit from you embracing it.

Here are some random things I have done through my journey to home in on my life's purpose and passion.

- Stop looking for your life's purpose and passion. Yes, stop. Sometimes your purpose just finds you as you embrace your moments in life well.

- Burn the box of any comfort zones you live in and try new things, new experiences. Your purpose may wait for you just outside that box.

- Listen to those around you. They may give you clues as to what you are good at and what may point you to your purpose in life.

- Volunteer in places doing things that bring you joy. You just might uncover a deeper life-passion and purpose.

- Ask yourself better questions. What is wrong with the world that I would like to change? What is something I would enjoy doing whether I got paid for it or not? What is something that would be a hill I would not only charge up, but I would be willing to die on?

I pray you know the purpose of your life. And if you don't, I pray you find the courage to try different things to uncover your purpose. As I said, you deserve it. Your spouse, your children, your community of family and friends deserve to experience your soul and story ignited with purpose and passion.

Embracing Light

- Find your place in life's symphony and embrace your part like that triangle player.

- View your life like the whistling trash collector. If you look for the bad around you, you will find it. If you look for the good, you will find it too. It is all about perspective.

- Authentic community is about the heart of the people, not that everyone looks, thinks, and acts as you do. The greatest expressions of a community are made up of a diverse mix of people committed to compassion and seeking common ground.

- Too many people in today's culture are all about building walls and retreating in fear. Be bold and courageous and, instead, build longer tables. Nurture the community around you.

- Be secure in communing with yourself so that you do not look to your community to fulfill things that are your responsibility. No other person can "complete" another.

- Whether you are introverted or extroverted, your soul is wired for belonging, to know acceptance. Knowing you have acceptance improves your mental and physical health.

- Love really is what it's all about. Sure, it can hurt sometimes. But never experiencing love hurts much worse. You were wired for it. Love others the way you deserve to be loved. Oh, and don't forget to strive to love yourself as well. What is something you love about yourself?

- You have a God-given purpose that you were wired for. What are your talents? What is your giftedness? What hill would you charge up and be willing to die for? Think about that thing that sets your soul on fire. Living in your purpose nurtures flow in all areas of your life.

15

DANCE

Embracing Flow in Connection

Learn the unforced rhythms of Grace.
—Eugene Peterson, The Message

Come on, now. Put down the book for a moment, stand up, and shake what the good Lord gave you, as my mom used to say. Who doesn't need more dancing in their lives? Okay, so this whole chapter is not just about actual dancing, but more about the metaphor of how life should be more of a dance.

First, let's talk about really dancing. And, before anyone tries to use the excuse that they can't dance or have no rhythm, this is not about winning a contest; this is about enjoying the physical and emotional benefits of moving your body to the beat of a favorite tune. Life can get crazy. You are pulled in every direction with responsibilities, putting out fires, and trying to keep your head above water. I want you to stop what you are doing for ten minutes a day, put on your favorite song, and move your body. Don't tell me you do not have ten minutes. That is less than one percent of your day.

Why, in a book about finding your light in the darkness, am I telling you to dance? Because ten minutes of dancing a day will

- give you a fresh perspective on whatever challenges you are facing,

- flush the stress hormone, cortisol, out of your body,

- fill your body with all the feel-good hormones,

- help give you a hard reset emotionally (since motion and emotion are connected in our bodies),

- improve your physical health, and

- make you smile. I guarantee you cannot dance for ten minutes and not smile.

I had a client once give me an excuse. "If you knew the crazy life I have right now, you would not be telling me to dance. I do not have a spare minute in my day."

"You have shared much of your current life situation with me, and I am here to say you could use twenty minutes of dancing a day," I responded as lovingly as I could.

Eventually, both the husband and wife made dancing once a day a part of their self-care regime and saw much success in improving their life and outlook on things. Besides, most of us take life too seriously. Even as grown adults, our souls long for a little whimsy. I promise you it will improve the way you think and feel about life. No one wants to live life as a death march, checking boxes and putting out fires until they die. Enjoy life. Embrace your moments.

Now I will address the metaphor that life is a dance. The quote for this chapter furnished me with four words that helped me reframe the way I embrace life: *learn, unforced, rhythms,* and *grace.*

Learn—For so long, I separated my life between things being a complete success or a complete failure. I would not allow myself any middle ground. If I failed, I hated myself and wallowed in my worthlessness. If I succeeded, and I mean a complete success without qualification, I allowed myself to celebrate, but not for too long. I was terribly hard on myself. Coming to the realization that we all control only two things in life—our choices and how we respond to everyone else's—I had to come to view my life differently if I were ever going to find freedom. So, here's what I said to myself: *Okay, Travis, you are no longer driven by only success and failure. Instead, you are going to view both as learning opportunities. If you succeed, reinforce what you learned to achieve it. If you fail, it is a new learning opportunity for how not to do something.* In other words, I cut out the negativity and looked for opportunities to learn and grow.

Unforced—This is where the dancing comes in, as well as any other self-care measures you can put in place. Do not let yourself believe you are too busy for self-care. If your life is that crazy, you need it even more. Those who depend on you deserve a healthy and fully present you. Remember what you control in life. Stop trying to fit square pegs into round holes, thinking life will be better. Prioritize those things that must get done and those things you fully control. Then give yourself some time on things that you influence and enjoy. Everything you do not control needs to be let go.

Rhythms—Life has a rhythm to it. You were wired for rhythm. I do not mean that you should order everything in life perfectly and have everything planned down to the minute. That adds stress and moves us further from having rhythm. Rhythm is about flow. Let your past moments be in the past. Do not *would've, could've,* or *should've* yourself to death. Let your future moments stay in your future. Do not *what-if* yourself to death. Beauty and fulfillment, in this life, are not something we only experience when we reach the goal or hit the finish line. Do not live for the end goal or even for the weekend. Beauty is found in your moments. The journey is about the steps you take. Live in your now, then plan your next best step and repeat. Having this attitude, my dad lived more life in six weeks during his cancer battle than some people live in six years.

Grace—Oh, how we all need grace. We are all flawed and imperfect and in need of some of that unmerited favor at times. I am not saying we should look past people's mistakes any more than we should look past ours, but we shouldn't camp there and get stuck by the fear and shame that we are messed up beyond repair. God does not leave us at the point of our greatest mistakes, so we should not do that to ourselves or others, either. Erring on the side of grace just might be the boost someone needs to find freedom from their burdens or darkness. We do not know the stories people are living. In a world where so many are treading water, let's connect with them by being a life vest and not a cement block.

Burn The Box

One thing that hinders our ability to connect well with others is letting our thoughts give way to stereotypes and assumptions. There isn't a lot I want to say about this other than to challenge you to just stop doing it. It is not only potentially painful and harmful to others, but it is harmful to you; it blocks you from the experience of community and connection that your soul longs for. Here is the deal about stereotyping: your observation might prove true on occasion, but most of the time, you will fall far short of truly understanding the person you are putting in that box. What you wouldn't want to be done to you, shouldn't be done to others. We are all so much more than the judgmental and predetermined snapshots of stereotypes that so many throw around.

As far as assumptions go, we all know that saying, right? I will not repeat it here, but suffice it to say, assuming is a lazy and judgmental habit. Whether it be in person or that hidden space behind the social media screen, take the time to go directly to whomever is about to be on the receiving end of your assumption, and seek the truth from their mouth. Do not take another person's word for it. Spreading rumors is as destructive as assuming, if not worse. If you do not want to face the person to seek the truth, then maybe the best thing to do is to let that thought or topic go.

You do not deserve to stay in bondage to doing things the way you always did them, especially when they are painful and destructive. Past experiences will often lead us to fall into the trap of conveniently putting people in boxes. Work to recognize where you may struggle with stereotyping and assuming and release that inner narrative. It will free you from a lot of stress and make life more joyful. Burn those boxes. And, while the fire is hot, be sure to burn the boxes we place ourselves in. Once I found freedom from my hacked narrative and limiting beliefs, I had a bonfire of boxes to burn. I learned we put people, situations, and ourselves in these convenient and limiting packages when we fear them or don't understand them. Until we recognize and challenge those narratives, we will lazily continue in those thinking patterns. Breaking those chains requires humility in acknowledging them, a vulnerability in getting the help needed to break them, and courage to follow through on the process. Your ability to connect with yourself and others will be so much richer in the freedom you will find.

It Is More Than Just Proximity

How well are you connected to others? I ask this question to a lot of clients, and here are some answers I get:

"Well, I have almost two thousand friends on social media."

"I work with an office of about forty people."

"We live in a really big neighborhood."

To all these answers, I respond, "That is great, but I asked how well you are *connected* to others." While many are blessed with rich connections in their lives, millions of people live mostly disconnected from those around them. They are immersed in the shadow world of social media, victims of the isolation 2020 brought us all, and living out their lives in quiet desperation. They may be surrounded by hundreds of people through work, church, and the streets they live on, but they are connection starved.

Being connected to others is not just about proximity. But what is it? If you read about it in psychology journals and other places, it seems to be a hard concept to nail down. But, to me, a connection is about a person awakening part of your soul in a way you want to be around them. Being connected to them awakens your internal sense of value. They add to your life. We can experience connection with others on an emotional, mental, spiritual, or physical level. Some connections entail several or all four of those. The depth of our connection is also not equated to how long you have known someone or how often you see them. I feel connected to someone when I am compelled to show compassion for them or if I feel led to support or help them in growing in their lives. I want to share three different groups that I feel deep compassion for to illustrate ways connections can happen in our lives. These are just some of my many experiences. There are countless ways to connect with others.

Joplin, Missouri—It was the summer of 2011. The costliest and one of the deadliest tornadoes in American history had hit the small town of Joplin on a sleepy Sunday evening. Having led multiple disaster-relief trips during the Hurricane Katrina cleanup, I was poised and ready to go help this town. I, and several friends, put the word out on social media, and within a week we had enough donations to fill two sixteen-foot trailers and thirty-six volunteers ready to go help. Unlike past trips, many people were going on this one that I did not personally know. We arrived in Joplin, and on the first morning, we set out on the perimeter of the damage zone to see who we could help.

During disasters, all the big relief agencies head to the center of destruction, so we tried to focus on the people who often feel forgotten and left out. One of the first families we found was a single mother and her two daughters. Their property was destroyed, and they were all alone trying to salvage what they could of their belongings before crews like ours tore the rest of the structure down. It is hard to explain what took place between the volunteers, this family, and all the others we helped. We instantly felt a comfort level with one another. We intimately shared about our lives; we grieved over loss; we sweated next to one another, and friendships were forged that remain in place ten years later. One way we make connections with others is through circumstances—in this case, a disaster.

In my experience, authentic connections with others are birthed when three things take place: sharing, caring, and repairing. We intimately shared our lives together in Joplin, albeit for one week. We offered caring compassion through the hard work of digging out of the disaster, sharing meals together, and listening to one another when we needed to process our feelings. We experienced repairing, through the physical labor we did alongside each other and in one another's hearts as we helped families cope with catastrophic loss. Meeting people at the point of their needs is one of the beautiful ways we make connections with our fellow human beings. May you find ways to meet the needs of others, and may your heart be enriched for it.

Table Fifteen—Igniting Souls Publishing Agency, which helped make this book possible, hosts a special conference every year in October. The first year I attended was 2019. I had high hopes of making connections that would help me publish my book and better build my coaching practice. I did not really have any deeper expectations since I only knew one person out of the four hundred or so that would be in attendance. I was instantly amazed by how friendly and compassionate every single person was that I crossed paths with. At the opening event of the conference, there was a huge room with multiple tables of ten chairs each. I had met two people only moments before, so we decided to sit at a table together. It slowly filled up and the ten of us began sharing our names, where we were from, and what our goals were for the gathering—you know, typical conference small talk. As the different speakers and events moved on, something began to happen at our table. We all went from being random strangers brought together by an event to building intimate connections with one another over our shared passion for writing, speaking, and coaching. We found common ground, and we embraced it with one another. That is another way strong, intimate connections are birthed. We experienced the vulnerability of sharing our hopes, dreams, and failures together. The caring compassion for one another became palpable, and it started feeling like we had known each other for years. There was repairing in one another's lives taking place as one person would share an area of struggle, another would share how they had gained a victory in that area. It was a beautiful expression of connecting with our shared passion for bettering ourselves through writing and coaching. It is about to be two years since that gathering, and table fifteen members still meet through Zoom™ to catch up with one another at least once a month.

The neighborhood—So we have talked about making connections with others through circumstances and common ground, and now the third area is community. We live out in the country on a very long private driveway shared by several other families. We each own between two and ten acres of land. Before moving to this property, about seven years ago, we only knew one of the six families in our little community. Everyone was friendly when we moved here—you know, no one egged each other's houses, and we waved as we passed one another. But that quickly changed soon after settling in. We began meeting in each other's yards, helping meet small needs around each other's homes, and soon we began experiencing the richness of truly authentic connections. We are now all like one big family. We feed each other's pets, share meals, meet each other at the point of need, and help care for each other when one of us is sick. I would love to see this happen in every neighborhood across the country. What is special about our little neck of the woods? Nothing really, except everyone here has open and vulnerable hearts; we trust one another, and we genuinely feel safe and loved by each other. Each of our lives is the richer for it.

Hey, I Know You

So, what do you need to do to experience the richness of authentic connections with others, to live life like the dance it is supposed to be? First, do the work to be sure you are connected to yourself. It may sound crazy, but I cannot tell you how many times I see a client's thinking vapor-locked by asking them, "How well do you know yourself?" I am convinced one of the reasons we fail to connect well with others and thrive in a vibrant community with one another is because we really do not know our own selves well enough. That is what awakening to your internal narrative is all about.

We must learn to sit regularly with ourselves and just listen. I know it can be uncomfortable, especially for those who hold on to burdens of unresolved trauma, fear, or anxiety. Use the QEDLG (question, explore, discover, learn, grow) line of self-questioning and scan your body physically and emotionally as you do. If you feel something, explore it, and seek to find the source. Allow yourself to feel and experience your feelings. No, they are not your truth in and of themselves, but they do point you to areas of pain and dysfunction. In short, how do you get to know someone better? You spend time with them. That is what you must do: spend some time with yourself. You are never too busy to work on being whole and present.

One last thing that I love doing with clients that helps them hear their inner voice better is something I call "random-word journaling." Think of a random word, any word that comes to mind. Write it down at the top of the page. Now, write one full page about that word with whatever thoughts come to mind. Do not worry about grammar and punctuation. Do not sit and think as if you were writing a paper for school. This is a free association exercise where you write what comes to mind without stopping until you fill the page. Then read it back to yourself to see what came out. It might surprise you. Does this sound weird? I promise you it will grow you in your ability to hear and respond to your inner narrative. Is your life more of a death march of responsibilities and tasks rather than a dance?

You deserve better. Work on connecting better to yourself and embrace opportunities to make connections with others. I would recommend getting an accountability partner and a journal for this. Oh, and remember to dance and embrace whimsy often. Life is short.

Embracing Light

- You have a better day when you add in a few minutes of dancing.

- Your life rhythm is only found in one place, your present moments. Do not let your past or your future rob you of the beautiful experience of your present.

- We live in a world where many people are barely treading water. Be sure your presence is like a life vest and not a cement block.

- Burn the boxes of limitations you place on yourself and others. Embrace the life around you anew each day. Be careful to not let stereotypes and assumptions rob you of amazing connections with others.

- Embrace a little whimsy in your life. There is no need to be serious twenty-four hours a day.

- Look for opportunities to connect to others through circumstances, common ground, and in the community where you live.

- Intimate connections with others are like oxygen to your soul.

- Above all else, work hard to know yourself.

16

STORY

Embracing Flow in Creation

To practice any art, no matter how well or badly,
is a way to make your soul grow. So do it.
—Kurt Vonnegut

It bears repeating; you carry all the light you will ever need to illuminate all the darkness you will ever face. Okay, so this chapter may end up sounding like a raucous cheering section trying to encourage you to take the steps to pursue your best life—oh, who am kidding? That's partly what it is, but it is so much more than that. This chapter represents the culmination of my journey to find myself and freedom from forty years of darkness. It is filled with the experiences of my heart and the hope that you find something here to ignite your soul. This chapter will be a little different from all the others. I will share some new thoughts and revelations, but I also want to close out the book by repeating some reminders of the most profound things that helped me on my journey.

You—there truly is not another *you* in the universe. You are special and unique. You truly are enough. I know if you struggle with the bondage of past trauma, anxiety, or other mental health issues keeping you from realizing your full potential, this may be hard to believe. I feel you. I was there for a long time. People told me I was special, and I struggled to believe them. I knew what God said about me, and I struggled to believe that. The bondage of my internal narrative and those limiting beliefs had me thinking there was such a thing as brokenness that could never be repaired. That is a lie.

So, what makes you so special? First, God created you and loves you. But no matter what you have been through, you have unique giftedness that no other human ever has or ever will have. I learned there was even giftedness in my pain. What hurt me and scared me for so long are now things that I am blessed to use in connecting to others who are hurting in the same way. How cool is that?

We all have a story. Every thought, feeling, and experience is written in that story. Much of it is beautiful and fun to recall, but some of it we wish were not there. We cannot change our story, though. Every chapter, painful or joyful, makes us who we are. Every good thing and every bad thing can be used to teach us and grow us if we only believe. Think of this: no one has lived your exact story from your exact perspective, ever. All your experiences absorbed into your consciousness create a view of life no one else has ever had. Therefore, I tell people all the time, "The world needs your story!" We need your perspective. No one can shine the light of hope and freedom as you can. If you are reading this, and you do not feel hope, freedom, or joy, then please talk to someone. You may contact me if you like. Freedom is yours for the taking. Oh, how I wish someone would have told me that thirty or forty years ago.

Maybe you are reading this and thinking *Travis, you don't get it. You do not know my story. I have made too many mistakes and felt too much pain to ever deserve to be free and joyful.* Oh, dear friend, I know how you feel. If you get nothing else from this book, hear this. I swore I was worthless and could never experience the hope and joy those around me had. I told a counselor in Minnesota I had screwed my whole life up. I had ruined all the good I had accomplished. All the things God did in and through me were wasted. He grinned and told me, "Well, congratulations, friend; you are now more powerful than God." At first, I wanted to punch him. But he explained, "If you can live a life that God cannot redeem, then wouldn't that make you more powerful than He?" He had a point. What I learned there, I now see as a paramount truth that could help millions find freedom from their hurts and struggles if they would only believe. Friend, you cannot live a life that God cannot or will not redeem if you only believe and allow Him to do it. Remember, God does not leave you at the point of your greatest failure or mistake, so do not let your inner voice or someone else force you to stay there, either.

Don't Be the Dead Sea

The reason a lot of people live in bondage to their hacked narrative is that they do not believe they have anything to offer the world around them. Even if I do not know you, I can tell you this is not true. You are creative. You have gifts and abilities, some even born out of your struggles. See, the world lulls many of us into becoming silent consumers of life. Sit back, take it all in, and don't create any waves. Advertising, television shows, movies, and music all tell us to get this, buy this, consume this, and you will be happy. But we were not made to be consumers. We were made to be creators, to give of ourselves to the world around us. We were created to love others through the sharing and giving of our stories to the world. The reason so many people are unhappy and living lives of hopelessness and quiet desperation is that they have become like the Dead Sea.

The Jordan River is rich and full of life. It flows into the Sea of Galilee and the Dead Sea. The same river feeds both bodies of water. While the Sea of Galilee is vibrant and full of life, the Dead Sea is devoid of life. Why is that? Because the Sea of Galilee receives the water from the Jordan and then gives it back out to continue flowing. The Dead Sea receives water from the Jordan, but there is no outlet, so nothing flows from it. It is the same for us humans. Those people I have met who are the fullest of life receive from the world around them, but they also give to others. Those who live lives of hopelessness, thinking they have no value and nothing to offer the world, are like the walking dead.

You Are Creative

I have heard a lot of people say, "I have nothing to offer the world. I am not creative. I cannot make anything. I have no talent to write, paint, or play a musical instrument." Okay, if that were the scope of being creative, then I can see how it might be true. But guess what? You are creating every minute you live and breathe. You may not be painting or writing a song, but you are writing the story that is you. As you interact with others, you are giving from the story of you.

One of the things my dad enjoyed doing most was working with his best friend to build wheelchair ramps for those in need. They did this for several years and blessed people all over our city. My dad was an extremely talented, self-taught carpenter. Besides ramps, he also enjoyed building bluebird houses and giving them away. He truly had the gift to create, but the most creative thing I ever witnessed him doing was giving himself to people around him. I could share countless stories, but one simple act stands out in my heart more than others. He and his friend were building a ramp for a lady about twenty-five miles outside the city. She was an elderly lady that lived alone in an old mobile home. There was no one else around for several miles. She needed the ramp to be able to get out of the house to get to medical appointments.

On the last day there, my dad noticed her struggling with something on the front porch. She was trying to open a can of beans with what my dad described as a hand-crank can opener that looked like it came from the 1940s.

He walked over and opened it for her. She replied, "Thank you so much. Somedays I cannot even open these cans, and I have to just eat what I have." She said the food bank that often brought her food gave her a lot of cans that didn't have the flip-open lids. My dad was moved by that moment. The next day, he went to the store, picked up a nice electric can opener and drove back out to her house, and gave it to her. She wept and said it was the nicest thing anyone had done for her in years. A simple act? Sure, it was. But it was also a beautiful picture of someone giving their love away, shining a light into someone's darkness or struggle. That is the creating we were made for. If you do more and can paint, build, play an instrument, or any other traditional form of creating, that is great. How are you using it to give to the world around you? The world needs you and your story. Get creative in giving yourself away to others. It will build you up in the process. You will be more joyful, more at peace, and more in love with your life.

The Crescendo

Here is where we leave it all on the table. We are nearing the end of our journey together. But I do hope we cross paths in some way in the future. I pray this book has blessed you in some way. Before we go, I want to pour out all that has been stirring in my heart during this journey. May at least one of these nuggets help you wherever you are in your own journey. If you live in your light already, be bold and shine it brightly on all those you cross paths with. If you still struggle with darkness, reach out to someone, dear friend. No one can make the journey alone. Trust me, I tried doing that for a long time.

- Never stop chasing your passion. What sets your soul on fire? What stirs you in a way you cannot let go of it? Find a way to connect to that in your daily life.

- You do not have to have every step of the journey figured out before you move. Too much order in things can stifle the creative process. Just focus on taking your best next step and repeat.

- Be intentional with your life, your thoughts, feelings, emotions, and those around you. You either write your story or it will write you.

- Be here now. You can only truly live in this present moment.

- Do not fear your future and the blank pages of your story. Rather, fear continuing to write the same thing over and over. Change starts on the page you are on.

- If your safe space, whether literally or figuratively, causes you fear or pain, it may be a prison instead of a safe space.

- Free yourself from complaining. It wastes so much beautiful energy you could be using for good. Complaining is like trying to dip water with a fishnet—a lot of effort and little to show for it.

- What do you fear most in life? The answer to that could hold the key to all the freedom and healing you long for. Run straight into your fears. The minute you face your fear, it begins to die.

- Asking for help is not a weakness. It is one of the strongest things you can do.

- Vulnerability is strength. It fuels movement, change, and growth.

- Brokenness is the backbone on which the courage to move forward begins.

- Do not fear pain, physical or emotional. It is trying to tell you there is something that needs help and your attention.

- Hating yourself is destructive. Give yourself grace. Look for the best. If you cannot accomplish this on your own, get help from a trusted friend or professional.

- Shame offers you nothing good. It tells horrible lies and keeps you in bondage to your greatest pain or mistake.

- You cannot time-travel, so stop letting your mind and emotions do it. Raise awareness to the *would've*, *could've*, and *should've* narrative that keeps you focused on the pain and regret of your past. Notice the *what-if* narrative that keeps you stressed and anxious about your future. Be present-focused. Now is the only place you can truly live. It is the only place you can encounter God.

- *Always* and *never* are never always true. Terminal language is rarely ever purely true and causes distress in communication, whether it be with others or yourself.

- Drop the masks. Destroy the facades. They waste your precious energy. Be you and let those who embrace you do so and release those who do not. You will never please the whole world, and you could lose yourself by trying.

- Strive for flow in all you do. Seek clarity and focus on whatever you pursue. Embrace the moment you are in fully. Be joyful.

- Our narrative and hacked beliefs help create the monsters in our heads. Knowing that gives us the power to defeat them. Never give up; never quit until you are free from your darkness and pain. I believe in you.

- No story cannot be redeemed for good if you only believe.

- Wake up every day with the prayer, "God, show me the world through your eyes and help me to be a better version of myself.

- Do not ride the waves of others but create your own waves. You are God-wired to be creative. Discover what brings you joy.

- Be the source of what you feel the world needs.

- Embrace life tightly and find joy in all your moments. Be like the whistling trash collector and the triangle player.

- Never give up. Be tenacious in the pursuit of your passions. My dad built a pond with a box blade; you can do whatever you set your mind to.

- Do not waste your life chasing the perfect moment. Instead, live perfectly in every moment you have.

- Use the QEDLG (question, explore, discover, learn, grow) method often. Ask deep probing questions but never accept the easy answers. Pursue excellence in all you do.

- You are the only you the world has. We need your story. We need your light.

- Never stop imagining. It is the playground of the mind where greatness is born. Jesus instructed us to come to Him as children. Be awed by the world around you. Be curious.

- Embrace self-care. You do not go on a long journey in a barely working vehicle, so stop going through life running on fumes and with loose lug nuts.

- Words create worlds. Awaken to the internal narrative of your story.

- Wherever you are, be all there.

- Go to that good HELL daily. *Hug* someone. Make *eye contact* with others. *Laugh* often. *Listen* well.

- Be the third frog on the lily pad. Set your sights on your goals, and then put all your efforts on the jump to the next lily pad. You will get there. Patience is a virtue.

- Be still. Take ten minutes a day to sit still, breathe, and listen.

- Dance. Oh, please never stop dancing. Every life needs a little whimsy.

- What are you thankful for? Name three things every day and ask yourself why you are thankful for those things.

- Be a warrior and not a worrier.

- We are *all* fireflies. *You* are a firefly.

You carry all the light you will
ever need to illuminate
all the darkness you will ever face.

NOTES

1 Anderson, T. Carlos "Tim". (2019 August 19). Words Create Worlds. *The T. Carlos Blog.* (from *The Austin American-Statesmen*-2019, August 18). Retrieved from https://justalittlebitmorebook.com/2019/08/19/words-create-worlds/.

2 Cuncic, Arlen. (2021, May 27). What is Shame. *Very Well Mind.* Retrieved from https://www.verywellmind.com/what-is-shame-5115076.

3 Young, Danielle. (2020, June 12). Trauma and the Brain: Signs You Might be Living in Survival Mode. *Child Guidance Resource Center.* Retrieved from https://cgrc.org/blog/trauma-and-the-brain-signs-you-might-be-in-survival-mode/.

4 Nunez, Kirsten. (2020, February 21). Fight, Flight, or Freeze: What This Response Means. *Healthline.* Retrieved from https://www.healthline.com/health/mental-health/fight-flight-freeze.

5 Schneider, Tobias Van. (2017, June 22).. If You Want it, You Might Get it. The Reticular Activating System Explained. *Desk of Van Schneider Blog.* Retrieved from https://medium.com/desk-of-van-schneider/if-you-want-it-you-might-get-it-the-reticular-activating-system-explained-761b6ac14e53.

6 Brasil, Addison. (2020, November 16). How I Learned the Difference Between Thoughts and Feelings. *Tethr Blog.* Retrieved from https://www.tethr.men/content/founders-thoughts-how-i-learned-the-difference-between-thoughts-and-feelings.

7 Bancroft, Courtney, MA-LCMHC. (2017, April 5). The Connection Between our Thoughts, Feelings, and Behaviors: Part 1. *Carolina Pediatric Therapy*. Retrieved from https://www.carolinapeds.com/blog/2017/04/the-connection-between-our-thoughts-feelings-and-behaviors.

8 Barkman, Robert, PhD.. (2021, May 19). Why the Human Brain is so Good at Detecting Patterns. *Psychology Today*. Retrieved from https://www.psychologytoday.com/us/blog/singular-perspective/202105/why-the-human-brain-is-so-good-detecting-patterns.

9 Moore, Catherine. (2021, October 19). What is Flow in Psychology? Definition and 10+ Activities to Induce Flow. *Positive Psychology*. Retrieved from https://positivepsychology.com/what-is-flow/.

10 Wildenberg, Lori. (2021, September 13). What are the Seven Deadly Sins? *Crosswalk*. Retrieved from https://www.christianity.com/wiki/sin/what-are-the-seven-deadly-sins.html.

11 Hani, Julie. (2017, August 8). The Neuroscience of Behavior Change. *Startup + Health*. Retrieved from https://healthtransformer.co/the-neuroscience-of-behavior-change-bcb567fa83c1

12 Soroski, Jason. (2021). The Book of Haggai. The Online Community of *Christianity.com*. Retrieved from https://www.christianity.com/bible/niv/haggai/.

This book is dedicated to:

-My Mom and Dad, who did not live to see this dream come to life. Your legacy has been, and always will be, written on my soul.

-My wife and children (Regenea, Amanda, and Joshua) who have shown me unconditional love and support throughout my journey, especially in my quest for freedom and healing.

-To my Igniting Souls Publishing family/tribe. Your encouragement has always been breath to my soul. A special thanks to my friend, Brenda Haire, for igniting this spark inside me, and to my Publisher, Kary Oberbrunner for helping to fan that spark into a flame.

ABOUT THE AUTHOR

Travis M White is a soul on fire. Through his coaching, writing, and speaking, he helps individuals, families, and groups discover and overcome limiting beliefs and destructive internal narratives keeping them from experiencing their best life.

Travis wrestled with finding himself for much of his life as he secretly dealt with the effects of childhood sexual abuse. The fear and shame of believing he was worthless and unlovable resulted in struggles with drugs and alcohol, a suicide attempt, and poor choices that would test the limits of his relationships with others, as well as his own self-belief.

Today, Travis lives a joyful and transformed life as he uses his experience and training to help others master their own internal narratives. His desire is that the work he does will help others overcome the bondage of past pain and trauma while avoiding the many pitfalls he endured. He, and his wife Regenea, live in East Texas, where they enjoy a thriving coaching practice. When not working with others they enjoy spending time with their adult children, Amanda, and Joshua, their many pets, and the countless people they are blessed to call friends.

Connect at integrativenarrativecoaching.com

Integrative Narrative Coaching

Professional Coaching for Life, Career,
Relationships, and Trauma Recovery

Want to work with Travis, or his wife
Regenea, contact us at:

integrativenarrativecoaching.com
Email: travismwhitecoach@gmail.com

Available Services:
1-1 coaching (in person or video), intensives,
self-paced courses, masterclasses, speaking
engagements, and membership opportunities

Got a story inside you?

Author Academy Elite could be the right choice for helping you write, publish, and market your book.

Discover more at:

https://vt226.isrefer.com/go/aaevtrng/travismichaelwhite/

Made in the USA
Monee, IL
23 January 2022

88852240R00128